ABOUT TH

CW00848408

Killian H. Gore was born in Fort Phantom in Texas in 1976. He is a distant relative of the serial killer Ellen Mort who was born in Liverpool, England and later vanished in Salt Lake City, Utah, after violently butchering all five of her husbands.
He is the author of the short story collection Before Halloween as well as the novellas Beyond Bigfoot, The Thingy From Another World and The Demon of Heritage and the quiz books The Unauthorized Friday the 13th Quiz Book and The 'Burbs Unauthorized Quiz Book. His first screenplay, Blood Stained Windows, is currently being produced by Snowy Morning Movies.

He lives in Warrington, England.

www.facebook.com/killianhgore
www.twitter.com/killianhgore

Incredible Horror Movie Facts

by Killian H. Gore

Also by Killian H. Gore

Before Halloween
The Thingy From Another World
Beyond Bigfoot
The Demon of Heritage

Non-Fiction:

The Unauthorized Friday the 13th Quiz Book
The 'Burbs Unauthorized Quiz Book

Screenplays:

Blood Stained Windows

Contents

Foreword

Hello fellow horror fans! You've made a very wise choice in purchasing this book - *trust me!* I've searched high and low for the many weird, crazy, shocking, unbelievable, funny, spooky, interesting, strange, scary and just downright incredible stories featured within. I like to think I've concocted a great blend of some well-known tales, some lesser-known ones as well as a number of exclusives ones that I've had the privilege of uncovering by some famous folk in the world of horror - just for this book and just for you!

I believe what actually got me started off was the story of Mercedes McCambridge, the voice of Panzuzu in *The Exorcist*. It was so long ago that I can't quite recall where I heard about the unfortunate events surrounding the death of McCambridge's son but it struck me that it would be an interesting concept for a book. Initially I had called it "Strange Movie Facts" but after many months of research I thought that "Incredible" was a much more fitting word.

I sincerely hope that the facts I've collated for this book will be as interesting to you as they are to me. If you've heard some of them before (and if you're a horror movie fan like me, then you've probably encountered a fair few of them over the years) I hope that you will, at least, enjoy reading them as part of a much bigger collection. And it is, I must say, a collection that I am very proud of.

So, let's begin!

8

Incredible Horror Movie Facts

Alien (1979 – Directed by Ridley Scott)

Scriptwriter Dan O'Bannon was down on his luck when he conceived the idea for *Alien*. At the time he was living at Ronald Shusett's house and was desperate to no longer be sleeping on his friend's sofa. The two of them got together to write the screenplay for *Alien* and were surprised at the positive reaction it received from the studios after they sent it out. But they knew the Hollywood system well enough to know that projects can easily fall apart, "Everything had fallen through for us. Nothing had ever worked," O'Bannon said. Even after they received their first paycheck they continued to be pessimistic. Fortunately sci-fi was hot in Hollywood at the time, owing to the massive success of *Star Wars,* and the project continued to expand, "We caught this science fiction boom just right... our script was on the market just a month after *Star Wars* was released."

O'Bannon has said in early interviews that producers David Giler and Walter Hill only wanted to give him a story-writing credit in the finished film, claiming that they had extensively re-written the original screenplay. It appears that their motivation was simply to steal the credit from rookies O'Bannon and Shusett. The producers clearly had a change of heart throughout the lengthy production process and O'Bannon would be given sole writing credit with Shusett receiving co-story credit with O'Bannon.

Whilst shooting the classic chest-burster sequence, director Ridley Scott thought the best way to get a realistic reaction from his actors was to not tell them exactly how intense (and bloody) the effect was going to be. Actress Veronica Cartwright's (Lambert) performance perfectly captures her surprise and horror as the gory scene unfolded before her eyes - and all over her face!

John Hurt had initially been considered for the role of Kane but a scheduling conflict meant that they had to cast actor Jon Finch instead. Hurt was supposed to be filming *Zulu Dawn* (1979) in South Africa, although he was denied entry into the country when they confused him with actor John Heard (who was banned from South Africa for his political views). The weekend that Hurt returned to London he was informed that Jon Finch had been taken seriously ill. Ridley Scott immediately got in touch with Hurt to ask him if he wanted the part and Hurt was on the set the following morning, albeit very tired!

The working title for the script was *Star Beast*. In footage from the making of the movie the clapperboard can sometimes be seen to read *The Alien*.

The writers of the movie never intended for Ripley to be female – during the early stages of pre-production John Travolta was considered for the role.

Aliens (1986 – Directed by James Cameron)

Gordon Carroll, one of the executive producers on *Aliens*, says that James Cameron's pitch for the movie was as simple as walking up to a chalkboard, writing the word 'alien' and adding an 's' – to which he then drew a line through to make '$.' Oh, and he had just made a little film called *The Terminator*, so that may have swung it for him!

Tip Tipping, who starred as Pvt. Crowe, was also a very well respected stunt performer in films such as *Indiana Jones and the Temple of Doom* (1984), *Batman* (1989) and *Robin Hood: Prince of Theives* (1991) as well as a couple of the Bond movies. Sadly in 1993 he was filming the BBC television show *999* (about real-life accidents) when his parachute failed to open and he tragically plunged to his death.

Alien 3 (1992 – Directed by David Fincher)

Michael Biehn was paid more for *Alien 3* than he was for *Aliens* – even though he doesn't actually star in it! The money he received was merely for the use of his photograph that featured at the beginning of the movie.

Actor Charles S. Dutton, who played the inmate Dillon, was charged and convicted of the death of a man he got into a fight with when he was 17 years old. He served seven years in prison for manslaughter and only a few months after being released he was charged with possession of a deadly weapon and sentenced to three more years in prison. Maybe he was just getting into character for *Alien 3*?

With it being director David Fincher's debut feature film, the executives at Fox kept a very close eye on the young director during production. It was clearly the cause of much friction on set. In the documentary chronicling the making of the movie, *Wreckage and Rage*, Fincher grabs a boom microphone and says into it, "It's amazing to me that Fox is the number one studio in the country because they're all such a bunch of morons." This scene had initially been omitted from the *Alien Anthology* DVD box-set release but was restored for the Blu-ray version – along with over twenty minutes of other excised footage featuring Fincher's difficulties on set.

An American Werewolf in London (1981 – Directed by John Landis)

The scene in which David and Jack are attacked on the moors was actually filmed on the grounds of Windsor Castle in Windsor Great Park.

After Michael Jackson saw the movie he fell in love with it so much that he hired director John Landis and special effects make-up artist Rick Baker to work on his *Thriller* video. John Landis's wife, Deborah, designed Jackson's now iconic red costume for the video. Only two of the jackets were ever made, one of which recently sold at auction for $1.8 million. Deborah Nadoolman Landis is also notable for creating the fedora and jacket for Indiana Jones in *Raiders of the Lost Ark*.

The Amityville Horror (1975 – Directed by Stuart Rosenberg)

Peter O'Neill Jr. who lived in the real Amityville house between 1987 and 1997 was one of the victims of the September 11 attacks in 2001. The 21 year old was training to become a bond trader at his Uncle's firm, Sander O'Neill & Partners on the 104th floor of Tower Two.

The original film has spawned thirteen sequels to date – a lot of which seem to have nothing to do with the original storyline and film: *Amityville II: The Possession* (1982), *Amityville 3-D: The Demon* (1983), *Amityville 4: The Evil Escapes* (1989), *The Amityville Curse* (1990), *Amityville 1992: It's About Time* (1992), *Amityville: A New Generation* (1993), *Amityville Dollhouse: Evil Never Dies* (1996), *The Amityville Horror* (2005), *The Amityville Haunting* (2011), *The Amityville Asylum* (2013), *Amityville Death House* (2015), *The Amityville Playhouse* (2015) and *Amityville: The Awakening* (2015).

Anaconda (1997 – Directed by Luis Llosa)

Whilst shooting the film a power surge caused one of the massive animatronic snakes to go completely out of control, thrashing around as if it were a real anaconda. Actor Ice-Cube (Danny Rich) said that, "It was like fantasy and reality merging." The cameras were actually rolling at the time but they cut when they realized that the snake had gone completely loco – however, the filmmakers did include some of the footage in the finished film.

Actor Eric Stoltz (Dr. Steven Cale) has said that he didn't really have a fear of snakes before working on the movie - that was until he encountered a real 15-foot anaconda on the balcony of the hotel he was staying at whilst shooting the film in Brazil.

In 2014 wildlife expert Paul Rosolie announced that he was going to allow himself to be eaten alive by a giant anaconda whilst wearing a specially constructed protective suit. After all the hype surrounding the Discovery Channel show (*Eaten Alive*) viewers were disappointed to witness Rosolie merely wrestle with the snake for a minute or two before complaining that his arm was hurting. After viewers had waited for almost two hours for the big event, Rosolie was quickly pulled away from the snake and the whole debacle was quickly aborted. Disgruntled viewers quickly took to Twitter to voice their opinion that the program was all a big hoax.

Annabelle (2014 – Directed by John R. Leonetti)

The real Annabelle doll is quite unlike the one featured in both *The Conjuring* and *Annabelle*, although the stories connected to her are equally as chilling. The doll, which is actually a Raggedy Ann doll, is currently housed at the Warren Occult Museum in Connecticut, USA. It resides in a specially built cabinet with a holy cross above it and the words, 'Warning – Positively do not open' written upon it. The doll was said to be possessed by a deceased 7 year old girl called Annabelle Higgins and would often be found in different rooms or positions around the house. Notes were mysteriously found in the handwriting of a small child and blood appeared on the doll's hands and chest. It was only when the doll physically attacked someone that the famed paranormal investigators Ed and Lorraine Warren (the Amityville and haunting in Connecticut investigations) were brought in to attempt an exorcism on the doll. They concluded that a demon inhabited the doll, not a young girl. It has been alleged that a man who taunted the doll at the Warren Occult Museum died in a motorcycle accident shortly after his visit.

Behind the Mask: The Rise of Leslie Vernon (2006 – Directed by Scott Glosserman)

The film contains multiple references to famous horror films, ranging from the subtle to the blatant. Of the more obvious is the appearance of actors Robert Englund (*A Nightmare on Elm Street*), Zelda Rubinstein (*Poltergeist*) and Kane Hodder (*Friday the 13th* Parts 7 through 10). Hodder is seen entering 1428 Elm Street - which was filmed at the actual Elm Street house location (1428 North Genesee Avenue West Hollywood, Los Angeles). *Behind the Mask* also contains references to:

Hellraiser - a Lament Configuration puzzle box is clearly visible on a table behind Leslie after dinner at Eugene and Jamie's house.
Halloween – A man dressed as Michael Myers gets out of a car and walks toward the diner; Robert Englund's character is dressed in almost exactly the same manner as Dr. Loomis (Donald Plesance); there's a sign for the Red Rabbit Pub behind Kelly as she gives a piece-to-camera (a reference to the Red Rabbit matchbook seen in *Halloween*).
The Evil Dead – the car at Eugen and Jamie's house is the same as Ash's 1873 Oldsmobile Delta car.

Friday the 13th – Leslie Vernon's real surname is revealed to be Mancuso, which is a reference to Frank Mancuso Jr. (the producer of many of the *Friday the 13th* movies).

The Shining – Robert Englund's character is named Doc Halloran after Dick Hallorann (Scatman Crothers). Also when Leslie is applying his make-up you can hear the song *Midnight, the Stars and You* performed by Al Bowlly – the same song plays at the climax of *The Shining*.

A Nightmare on Elm Street – there are two young girls playing jump rope in the background of one shot at the high school in the same manner as they do in the *Nightmare on Elm Street* movies.

I asked director Scott Glosserman for some more obscure references and he told me that the librarian's surname (Collinwood) is an homage to the family name in *The Last House on the Left* (1972) – Collingwood. He also told me that Zelda Rubinstein's librarian character wears a completely yellow outfit in the film as a reference to *The Shining* (1980), "Yellow foreshadows death in *The Shining* because it's the Native American color for sacrifice."

In July 2012 a Kickstarter campaign was launched to help raise funds for a sequel to the film called *Before the Mask: The Return of Leslie Vernon* (also known as *B4TM*). Various rewards were offered including premiere tickets, signed scripts, props from the film, executive producer credits as well as the opportunity to be killed in the movie! Unfortunately only $183,046 was raised of the $450,000 target and, so far, the film hasn't gone into production.

The Birds (1963 – Directed by Alfred Hitchcock)

Daphne du Maurier, the author of the book that the film is based on, is the cousin of the Davies boys, George, John, Peter, Michael and Nicholas who were the inspiration for J.M. Barrie's *Peter Pan*.

In 1994 a TV movie sequel with original star Tippi Hedren was produced called *The Birds II: Land's End*. Director Rick Rosenthal (*Halloween II* and *Halloween: Resurrection*) was so disappointed by the finished film that he disowned it and credited it to the Director's Guild of America's official pseudonym, Alan Smithee.

Black Christmas (1974 – Directed by Bob Clark)

In 2007, director Bob Clark was tragically killed along with his son in a head-on crash with a vehicle that had steered into the wrong lane. The driver of the other car, Hector Velazquez-Nava, was an illegal immigrant from Mexico who was driving without a license and was three times over the legal blood-alcohol level. He initially pleaded not guilty but later changed his plea to no contest – neither admitting nor disputing the charge. He was sentenced to six years in prison.

The Blair Witch Project (1999 – Directed by Daniel Myrick and Eduardo Sánchez)

Some people still believe the film to be a real documentary – I have actually encountered people myself who swear it's all true!

Even though the film only took eight days to film it ended up taking around eight months to edit together, owing to the huge amount of footage that had been shot.

When Artisan Entertainment picked up the movie for distribution they said they didn't like the film's ending. They gave Myrick and Sánchez $80,000 (more than the original entire budget for the film!) to shoot a different ending and despite shooting various alternatives featuring, amongst other things, Mike hanging and Mike levitating, the filmmakers much preferred their original ending with Mike simply standing in the corner facing the wall. The executives at Artisan reluctantly agreed but warned them their ending could cost them millions at the box office. The film went on to gross $248,639,099 worldwide.

After the release of the film the two directors seemed to completely disappear off the filmmaking radar before returning to direct films separate from each other in 2006/2007. Sánchez made *Altered* (2006), *Seventh Moon* (2008), *Lovely Molly* (2011) and *Exists* (2014) whilst Myrick directed *Believers* (2007), *Solstice* (2008) and *The Objective* (2008). There has also been talk of a third *Blair Witch* movie but, possibly as a result of the negative reception of *Book of Shadows: Blair Witch 2* (2000), a part 3 has yet to be green-lit. Myrick and Sánchez have discussed the possibility of a prequel featuring Elly Kedward (the Blair Witch herself), filmed as a period piece in black and white.

The Blob (1958 – Directed by Irvin Yeaworth)

Rather strangely in September 1950 the New York Times ran a story about four police officers in Philadelphia who reported witnessing a saucer shaped object gliding down to earth. Once it had landed they attempted to touch the purple-glowing UFO only to discover it was made of a goo-like substance. After twenty minutes or so the *blob* had completely evaporated. Amazingly enough the FBI were brought in to investigate but found nothing more than a spot on the ground by the time they arrived. The case was turned over to U.S. Air Force Intelligence but no further documentation of the incident was ever recorded.

Every year in Phoenixville, Pennsylvania, the Colonial Theater holds a three-day event called *Blobfest* in celebration of the movie. The Theater served as the location for the famous scene of people running, screaming from the building. One of the highlights of *Blobfest* is said to be the re-enactment of the run-out scene and tickets are limited to 350 if you wish to take part.

Bloodbath at the House of Dead (1984 – Directed by Ray Cameron)

Ray Cameron, the director of *Bloodbath at the House of Death,* is British comedian Michael McIntyre's father. Whilst growing up McIntyre had always believed that his father had died of a heart attack but in 2010 his step-mother, Holly Hughes, informed him that Cameron had committed suicide by shooting himself in his apartment in Hollywood in 1993. After Michael planned to take part in the genealogy TV series *Who Do You Think You Are?*

Holly realized she had to tell him the truth before the TV show unearthed Cameron's death certificate.

In Michael McIntyre's autobiography *Life and Laughing: My Story* he reveals that at the age of six he provided the voice for the alien in the *E.T.* spoof at the end of the movie, uttering the line, "Oh shit, not again" as the spaceship leaves without him.

Bloody Murder (2000 – Directed by Ralph Portillo)

In the UK *Bloody Murder* was released on DVD as *Scream Bloody Murder.* Its sequel, *Bloody Murder 2: Closing Camp,* was then released in the UK as *Halloween Camp*. There was then a UK DVD sequel called *Halloween Camp 2: Scream If You Wanna Die Faster* (2004) which was actually an unrelated horror film called *Adam & Evil (2004)*! In other words, the *Halloween Camp* film series doesn't really exist! Still, fingers crossed for *Halloween Camp 3: The search for another unrelated horror film!*

The Burning (1981 – Directed by Tony Maylam)

The Burning was the first feature film for future film and TV stars Fisher Stevens (*Short Circuit*), Jason Alexander (*Seinfeld*) and Holly Hunter (*The Piano*).

The music score is by keyboard legend Rick Wakemen of the progressive rock band *Yes*.

The film's boogeyman, Cropsy, is based on a real upstate New York urban legend called 'Cropsey' – a campfire horror story that became popular in American Summer Camps in the 60's and 70's. He was said to be an escaped mental patient who lived in an abandoned lunatic asylum in Willowbrook. Sometimes it was said he had a hook for a hand whilst others describes him as wielding an axe, depending on who was telling the story. Chillingly in 1988 a man called Andre Rand was arrested in Willowbrook for murdering twelve-year-old Jennifer Schweiger. Rand was also linked to a number of other disappearances of young children from the area and has been successfully convicted of kidnapping seven-year-old Holly Ann Hughes, whose body was never found. Maybe Cropsy was real all along?

The Cabin in the Woods (2012 – Directed by Drew Goddard)

Despite the movie being filmed in early 2009 it wasn't released until 2012 for a number of reasons including a thwarted attempt to convert it into 3D and financial difficulties with original distributor MGM. Initially its release date was set for 5th February 2010.

Fran Kranz, who plays the stoner character Marty, was the only actor not to disrobe for the lakeside-swimming scene – not because he refused to but because, according to the filmmakers, he was, "Ripped like the Lord Jesus himself" which was an appearance they thought would have totally ruined the character.

Fran Kranz had a real scare whilst shooting on location in Vancouver - he decided to go for a little run to work up a sweat and ended up running into a black bear! But because he was making a movie his initial reaction was that the bear was only a man in a suit! When he realized it was real he promptly ran away screaming, "Bear, bear!"

In April 2015 author Peter Gallagher filed a $10 million copyright infringement lawsuit against the makers of the film claiming that they had liberally plagiarized his 2006 self-published novel *The Little White Trip: A Night in the Pines*. Gallagher's book features five friends (three males and two females – the same as *The Cabin in the Woods*) who take a trip to a remote cabin in the woods and are terrorized by the cabin's previous owner who has killed his entire family. In the end it is revealed that they are being filmed and manipulated by people behind the scenes. Gallagher claims that even certain character names are incredibly similar to those in his book, for example Julie and Dura are called Jules and Dana in the film, and the cabin is called Brinkley Cabin in the book and Buckner Cabin in the film.

The film caused some controversy amongst horror fans but not in reference to the film itself but a review of the film by New York Observer critic Rex Reed. In the article he made numerous inaccurate observations clearly as a result of not actually watching the movie or at least not really paying attention whilst viewing it. Here's a few examples comparing his review with the actual film:

"... they encounter a cretin with rotting teeth and one eye" – The *cretin* (actor Tim de Zarn as the character Mordecai) doesn't have rotting teeth, and he has *two* eyes.

"... creaking door to a cellar of corpses" – Maybe the door creaks but there's no corpses down there!

"Vampires circle the moon and suck the hot stud's blood" – If you've actually seen the film you'll know that there are no vampires and the *hot stud* (Chris Hemsworth) is killed when he rides his motorcycle into the camouflaged force field surrounding the woods and cabin.

"... the reefer-smoking dufus, so stoned he has to struggle to make complete sentences" – The *reefer-smoking dufus,* Marty (Fran Kranz), doesn't struggle to make complete sentences - He's actually very smart and articulate.

"What they fail to notice is the hidden cameras" – Marty discovers the hidden cameras in the cabin. *Duh!*

"It's all part of an elaborate video game that allows paying customers to watch real people slaughtered" – *No! Just NO, Mr. Reed!* That isn't what it's all part of at all! I think Rex Reed needs to re-watch the movie, strapped to a seat with his eyelids forced open like Alex in *A Clockwork Orange*!

Cannibal Holocaust (1980 – Directed by Ruggero Deodato)

The death scenes in the film were considered so realistic that the film was seized by a local magistrate in Italy and director Ruggero Deodato was arrested for murder. To complicate matters further the filmmakers had made the actors sign an agreement to refrain them from giving interviews or doing any publicity – this was to heighten the realism that the events portrayed in the film had actually taken place. Deodato had to gather up the actors to appear on a television show to prove that it was all make-believe. Furthermore he had to explain in court how he had achieved the famous impalement special effect – which was as simple as the actress sitting on a bicycle seat with a balsa wood length of wood held in her mouth. All murder charges were subsequently dropped. He did, however, kill seven real animals whilst making the film (two monkeys, a coatimundi, a turtle, a tarantula, a snake and a pig). Though no charges were brought against Deodato for animal cruelty, the film has suffered at the hands of the censors all over the world as a result and many countries have banned it entirely.

Carrie (1976 – Directed by Brian De Palma)

In the 1980's a musical adaption of *Carrie* became one of Broadways most notorious flops. It officially opened on May 12th 1988, and closed on May 15th 1988, after only 16 previews and 5 performances. It is estimated that it lost almost $8 million. Furthermore, during a try-out run in Stratford-upon-Avon, England, actress Barbara Cook (in the role of Margaret White) was very nearly decapitated on opening night by an elaborate set-piece involving a staircase that descended from above the stage. Cook immediately (and quite understandably) quit the production – although she agreed to stay on until a replacement was found. Unfortunately for Cook she ended up completing the month-long run but wisely declined to return for the disastrous Broadway production.

Children of the Corn (1984 – Directed by Fritz Kiersch)

Considering the film is only based on a short story by Stephen King it has gone on to spawn seven sequels plus a 2009 TV movie remake. They are: *Children of the Corn II: The Final Sacrifice* (1992), *Children of the Corn III: Urban Harvest* (1995), *Children of the Corn IV: The Gathering* (1996), *Children of the Corn V: Fields of Terror* (1998), *Children of the Corn 666: Isaac's Return* (1999), *Children of the Corn: Revelation* (2001), *Children of the Corn* – TV movie remake for Syfy (2009) and *Children of the Corn: Genesis* (2011). A lot of the scripts for the sequels were said to be unrelated spec scripts that Dimension Films owned. To save money they were rewritten to reference the storylines and themes of the franchise.

Child's Play (1988 – Directed by Tom Holland)

The inspiration for *Child's Play* is purported to be a real-life possessed child's doll named *Robert the Doll*. Robert belonged to Florida painter and author Robert Eugene Otto who claimed that one of his family's servants placed a voodoo curse on his childhood toy. The doll would mysteriously move around the house and knock things over and even conduct conversations with the young Otto. Whenever anything happened Otto would claim, "Robert did it." His family believed it was the boy causing all the trouble in the house and based on Otto's Aunt's recommendation the doll was locked in a box in the attic. A day later Robert's Aunt was found dead in her bed. The doll currently resides at the Martello Gallery-Key West Art and Historical Museum in Florida. Allegedly Robert is said to be repeatedly found in abandoned rooms in the museum without explanation and sometimes has gone missing for days at a time.

Communion (1989 – Directed by Philippe Mora)

Whitley Strieber, the author of the 1987 book upon which the film is based, has maintained over the years that his alien abduction story is true. The book itself is labeled as non-fiction. Author William S. Burroughs (*Naked Lunch*) was so fascinated by Strieber's account that he paid Strieber a visit and concluded that he was, "Convinced that he's telling the truth."

Creature From the Black Lagoon (1954 – Directed by Jack Arnold)

There have been numerous attempts over the years to remake the movie involving some very notable filmmakers. In 1982 John Landis was interested in having original director Jack Arnold on board with British writer Nigel Kneale (Hammer's *The Abominable Snowman*) writing the screenplay. Despite the script being completed, the film was cancelled for budgetary reasons as a result of opting to shoot in 3D. Joe Dante was also interested in doing a 3D remake around the same time. In 1992 John Carpenter was working on a remake for Universal and in 1995 Peter Jackson was given the opportunity to direct a remake. In 1996 *Ghostbusters* director Ivan Reitman was preparing to remake it. In 2001 Gary Ross (who would go on to direct *The Hunger Games*) was signed on to remake it with his father Arthur A. Ross (co-writer of the original film). Perhaps the furthest anyone ever got was Breck Eisner (*The Crazies*) who went as far as having the boat set built and had spent six months working with Mark 'Crash' McCreery (*Jurassic Park*) on the design for the Gill-man creature. As of April 2015 they are reports that a remake is still in development and that actress Scarlett Johansson has been offered the role of Kay Lawrence.

Creepshow (1982 – Directed by George A. Romero)

The young boy at the beginning of the film is Stephen King's son Joe Hill who has gone on to become a horror writer himself - his books include *Heart Shaped Box*, *Horns* and *NOS4A2*. Apparently whilst on a break from shooting, King took his son to a nearby McDonalds covered in blood and cuts and bruises make-up. The joke backfired when it transpired a member of staff had called the police after sighting the pair.

In 2009 there was an attempt to bring back *Creepshow* in the form of a web-series capturing the style and spirit of the original film. The series was called *Creepshow Raw* and although 10 episodes were planned only one was ever made – a particularly fun and gory story featuring Michael Madsen called *Insomnia* about a drunken stepfather who is slaughtered by the monstrous creature that resides in his stepson's closet.

Dark Water (2007 – Directed by David Nerlich and Andrew Traucki)

The true story upon which the film is based is every bit as terrifying as the movie. In 2003 three young friends in the Northern Territory of Australia were attacked by a 13-foot saltwater crocodile as they washed their clothes in the Finniss River. 22-year-old Brett Mann was taken by the shoulders and pulled under the water by the croc, allowing his two friends time to escape and swim over to a nearby tree. Moments later they watched in horror as the croc re-emerged, holding their friend in its jaws before swimming off. It returned a few minutes later and began to swim around the tree in which they were perched. The killer croc remained below them all through the night and the two friends had to keep each other awake in case they fell into the water. Thankfully the police located the pair the following morning and they were helicoptered to safety.

Dawn of the Dead (1978 – Directed by George A. Romero)

In February 2015, 17-year-old Tarod Thornhill entered the Monroeville Mall in Pennsylvania (the shooting location for *Dawn of the Dead*) and began shooting at customers with a semiautomatic handgun. Thankfully no one was killed but three people were injured, one of them critically. Six weeks before the shooting a huge brawl had taken place in the mall involving over a thousand teenagers. As far as I know, no zombies were involved in the fight.

In May 2015 an online petition was launched in an attempt to save the small bridge in the Monroeville Mall that featured in the movie. Over the past 30 years the mall has been renovated many times and a lot of the original features that are prominent in the movie have gone. The bridge is one of the last true recognizable remnants from the location.

Dracula (1931 – Directed by Tod Browning)

During the late 1920's and early 30's it was quite common in Hollywood for foreign language versions of popular movies to be filmed using the same sets and costume. Many of these alterative versions were considered lost but George Melford's Spanish-language version of Tod Browning's *Dracula* was re-discovered in the 1970's and restored. It was filmed during the night in the same period that Browning was shooting his movie during the day. Certain film critics and fans maintain that it is a much better film than Browning's. This is quite possibly down to the fact that when the Spanish crew arrived in the evening they would watch the dailies from English-language version and would work out ways to shoot it better – using more creative camera angles and more effective lighting.

Eaten Alive (1977 – Directed by Tobe Hooper)

Tobe Hooper's disturbing horror movie about the psychotic proprietor of a dilapidated hotel who feeds his victims to his pet crocodile was inspired by the real-life serial killer Joe Ball (The Alligator Man), a Texan who murdered up to twenty young woman before feeding their remains to his five alligators that he kept in a pond on the grounds of his saloon, the Sociable Inn in Elmendorf, Texas.

The film has had many alternate titles including *Death Trap, Horror Hotel, Horror Hotel Massacre, Legend of the Bayou, Murder on the Bayou, Starlight Slaughter, Brutes and Savages* and *Slaughter Hotel*.

Eraserhead (1977 – Directed by David Lynch)

David Lynch refuses to reveal exactly how they created the baby special effect for the film and people have speculated that it is a skinned rabbit, cow, lamb or, most disturbingly of all, a human fetus. Cryptically Lynch has said, "It was born nearby" and, "Maybe it was found." I do hope he's joking!

Jack Nance, the star of *Eraserhead* and many other of Lynch's movies, died in very mysterious circumstances in California in 1996. He claimed to have been attacked outside a donut store by two young Hispanic men. His friends noticed he had a bruise under his eye as he told them about the incident over lunch. He later complained of a headache and returned to his home where he died the following morning. The cause of death was recorded as subdural hematoma caused by blunt-force trauma. A murder investigation was launched which ultimately found no evidence to back up Nance's story. To this day the circumstances surrounding his death remain a mystery.

Stanley Kubrick screened the movie for the cast and crew of *The Shining* to, "Put them in the mood."

The Evil Dead (1981 – Directed by Sam Raimi)

The cabin in Tennessee that was used for the majority of shooting on *The Evil Dead* has some very real and spooky stories associated with it. The filmmakers were told that it was haunted and that no one had stayed there for over 40 years. The Tennessee Film Commission informed them that the man who had built the cabin was placing the final brick on the chimney when a bolt of lighting struck him down dead. When Raimi and company arrived at the location they noticed that there indeed was one brick missing from the top of the chimney. Perhaps even more disturbing was the story of a young girl and her mother and grandmother who moved into the cabin when they had nowhere else to live in the 1920's. During a stormy night the little girl was awoken by the frightening weather and ran screaming into her mother's room only to find her dead. She then went to her grandmother's room and discovered that she too was dead. Both deaths were natural causes but the shock of finding both her relatives dead on the same night had caused the girl to go a little crazy over the ensuing years. Whilst the filmmakers were shooting at the cabin a pick-up truck traversed along the mud road to the location and the occupants asked if they had seen Abigail. When they asked who Abigail was they were informed that she was the girl whose mother and grandmother had died in the cabin back in the 20's. They said she was now in her 60's and whenever there was a storm she had a habit of wandering off into the woods and returning to the cabin to call out for her mother and grandmother. Furthermore, after filming was completed the cabin mysteriously burned to the ground.

Sam Raimi's 1973 Oldsmobile Delta 88 car made its first feature film appearance in *The Evil Dead*. As well as featuring in the *Evil Dead* sequels and the 2013 remake it has also been seen in Raimi's *Crimewave* (1985), *Darkman* (1990), *A Simple Plan* (1998), *The Gift* (2000), The *Spiderman* trilogy (2002 – 2007) and *Drag me to Hell* (2009). Its appearance in the western *The Quick and the Dead* (1995) was kept secret for many years until Bruce

Campbell revealed that a special covered wagon frame had covered the Oldsmobile in the film. Raimi had previously said, "It's hidden somewhere, only I know, I'll never tell!"

Evil Dead II (1987 – Directed by Sam Raimi)

In the first *Evil Dead* film Sam Raimi had featured a ripped-up poster of Wes Craven's *The Hills Have Eyes* - the imagery signifying that *The Evil Dead* was a much scarier film. Wes Craven "answered back" by featuring *The Evil Dead* on a television in *A Nightmare on Elm Street*, as well as a poster for *The Evil Dead* on a bedroom wall. Finally Sam Raimi responded by featuring Freddy Krueger's glove in *Evil Dead II*. The reference-war had begun when Wes Craven featured a ripped-up *Jaws* poster in *The Hills Have Eyes* thus giving Raimi the idea to do the same thing in *The Evil Dead*.

The distribution company at the beginning of the film (Rosebud Releasing Corporation) is completely fictional and *Evil Dead II* is the only movie to ever feature it. The film was actually distributed by De Laurentiis Entertainment Group but as they couldn't release an X-rated movie they had to create Rosebud Releasing Corporation. Sam Raimi and Bruce Campbell conceived the stop-motion animated logo used at the start of the film.

The DVD commentary for *Evil Dead II* is particularly notable for the filmmakers poking fun at their own movie. It features Sam Raimi, Bruce Campbell, Greg Nicotero and Scott Spiegel reminiscing about the shooting of the film whilst joking about some of the more ridiculous moments. A particular highlight is how they ridicule producer Robert Tapert – who can be seen in the background of one scene unsuccessfully attempting to open an airplane door – Sam Raimi jokes that Tapert is still there today!

The Exorcist (1973 – Directed by William Friedkin)

Perhaps the most well known of the cursed horror movies and, owing to the film's subject matter, quite justifiably so. There are said to be nine deaths associated with the production – some quite directly (54 year old actor Jack McGowran died shortly after filming) and some more indirectly (Max Von Sydow's brother died just before filming). The strangest incident during production was arguably the set mysteriously burning down overnight, promoting director William Friedkin to request that the set be exorcised. His request was declined out of fear of heightening anxiety.

The famously haunting image of the demon Pazuzu's ghostly white visage is actually portrayed by *Guiding Light* and *General Hospital* soap opera actress Eileen Dietz. The actress was also used in a number of other shots playing Reagan - most notably the crucifix masturbation scene. Dietz did not receive a screen credit for her work in the film – neither did any of the other performers who were associated with portraying Reagan including Mercedes McCambridge who provided the voice of Panzuzu.

John Markle, the son of Mercedes McCambridge, killed his entire family before killing himself in 1987. He had been fired from his job at Stephens and Company for mishandling funds on Friday the 13th November. A $5 million lawsuit was filed against both him and Mercedes McCambridge (though she was later cleared of any criminal activity). On the 17th of November, Markle murdered his wife Christine as well as his two daughters, Amy and Suzanne, whilst wearing a Halloween mask in their home in Little Rock, Arkansas. He then, rather unusually, placed two guns to his forehead and killed himself. In his suicide note he admitted responsibilities for his crimes. He had also left a long and very bitter letter to his mother, part of which read, "You were never around much when I needed you, so now my whole family are dead."

Initially a music score for the film was created and recorded by composer Lalo Schifrin (*The Amityville Horror*) but when William Friedkin heard it he went crazy and grabbed the tape and threw it out of the recording studio, into the parking lot saying, "That's where that music belongs." Schifrin, who was present at the studio with his wife, was fired on the spot. Friedkin himself would suggest using music from Mike Oldfield's *Tubular Bells* album.

During the scene in which Father Dyer gives the last rites to Father Karras, Friedkin wasn't convinced by Reverend William O'Malley's performance – he was a real priest after all and not an actor. Friedkin asked O'Malley if he trusted him – he said he did. Friedkin then slapped O'Malley hard across the face and the cameras began to roll. O'Malley's visibly shaking hands during the scene are said to be as a result of Friedkin's rather unconventional directing tactic.

The film was edited at 666 Fifth Avenue in New York City. Spooky!

Contrary to popular belief, *The Exorcist* was never actually banned by the British Board of Film Classification in Britain. The theatrical version had been passed uncut in 1974 with an X-rating. Warner Bros. themselves had opted to not submit the film for home video release as they wished to avoid it being banned and ending up on the notorious *Video Nasty* (Video Recordings Act 1984) list. Warner finally submitted the film in 1999, after James Ferman had retired (Ferman was notorious for banning and cutting films – he'd even made 24 cuts to *Raiders of the Lost Ark*!).

In 2012 a Japanese 'exorcist' was given the death penalty for murdering six of her cult followers that she had beaten to death in her so-called 'exorcism rituals'.

The Exorcist III (1990 – Directed by William Peter Blatty)

The first cut of the movie was missing one crucial element – an exorcism! At the cost of almost $4 million the producers had to almost completely reshoot the ending so that it featured an exorcism scene.

The Exorcist III was said to be one of serial killer Jeffery Dahmer's favorite movies. Apparently he also was a *Star Wars* fan – so he wasn't a complete horror freak!

Exorcist: The Beginning (2004 – Directed by Renny Harlin)

John Frankenheimer was originally hired to direct the film but left because of health problems. He died suddenly a month later.

The film's replacement director, Paul Schrader, was fired from the project having completed shooting on it. The producers disliked the film that he had made and hired Renny Harlin to almost completely reshoot the entire film. Schrader was eventually permitted to release his version entitled *Dominion: Prequel to The Exorcist*. William Peter Blatty (author and screenwriter of *The Exorcist*) called *Exorcist: The Beginning,* "The most humiliating professional experience" whilst he said of Schrader's *Dominion,* "It's a handsome, classy, elegant piece of work".

The Exorcism of Emily Rose (2005 – Directed by Scott Derrickson)

The film is loosely based on Anneliese Michel, a young German woman who was supposedly possessed by demons. Over sixty exorcisms were performed on Michel over a ten-month period during which the priests identified various demons including Judas Iscariot, Nero, Cain, Adolf Hitler and Lucifer. Recordings were made of the exorcisms and the tapes were said to feature human growls and throaty gurgles together with demon voices describing the horrors of Hell. Over the course of the exorcisms Michel had been gradually starving herself and on 1st July 1976, she died in her home. Her parents and two priests were found guilty of negligent homicide as a result of her ordeal.

Actress Jennifer Carpenter claimed that during the production of the film her radio would go off in the middle of the night. On one occasion it switched itself on, particularly loudly, playing Pearl Jam's *Alive* - at the part in the song with the lyric, "I'm still alive."

Extinction: Jurassic Predators (2014 – Directed by Adam Spinks)

Despite being set deep in the jungles of Peru the film was actually filmed in Wales in the UK. In trying to find out exactly where the filmmakers shot the movie I was told that it was classified!

Fire in the Sky (1993 – Directed by Robert Lieberman)

The film was based on the supposed real life UFO incident in which American logger Travis Walton was abducted by aliens on November 5th 1975, whilst out in the woods with his work mates. The story and the case are well documented in the media and Walton himself penned the book *The Walton Experience* that would go on to be adapted into the feature film. At the time Walton's logger colleagues were subjected to polygraph examinations and it was concluded by the police that they were telling the truth. However, in 2009, Travis Walton participated in the American game show *The Moment of Truth* in which he was asked if he was indeed abducted by a UFO in 1975. The result of the polygraph test was negative and Walton missed out on winning the $100,000 he stood to gain if his answered had been determined to be true. Walton responded with, "Polygraph is 97% accurate, not a 100."

Frankenstein (1931 – Directed by James Whale)

Boris Karloff has said that it was really make-up effects man Jack P. Pierce who created the Frankenstein monster and he was merely the animation in the costume. Pierce's iconic make-up design is synonymous with the visual appearance of Frankenstein's monster yet it differed considerably from the description in Mary Shelley's novel. Sadly Pierce's Hollywood career went on a downward spiral after studios began to favor a new generation of make-up artists who could apply effects much faster. When he died in 1968 in near poverty, almost completely forgotten by Hollywood, it was said that a mere four or five people were in attendance at his funeral. Thankfully these days he revered by the current crop of special effects make-up artists including Tom Savini, Greg Nicotero, Howard Berger and Rick Baker.

When Boris Karloff was informed his wife was giving birth he rushed from the set of sequel *Son of Frankenstein* (1939) in full Frankenstein make-up to the hospital. The incident inspired an episode of Steven Spielberg's *Amazing Stories* TV show entitled *Mummy Daddy.*

English born director James Whale was found dead in his swimming pool in 1957. His death had originally been thought to be accidental until a suicide note was revealed by his ex partner David Lewis many years after his death. It was said that Whale had left a copy of William Brinkley's novel *Don't Go Near the Water* on his bedside table.

Friday the 13th (1980 – Directed by Sean S. Cunningham)

Writer and director Sean S. Cunningham had advertised the film even before a script had been written. He was struggling to produce a hit film and after realizing the importance of movie names he began brainstorming titles until he hit upon *Friday the 13th*. He loved the title so much that he took out an ad in Variety over the Fourth of July Weekend containing the title in big block letters, smashing through glass with the tagline, "The Most Terrifying Film Ever Made!" Proving that a mere title was enough to sell a movie, he began getting calls from distributors from all over the world who said they'd love to see the movie.

The Camp Crystal Lake setting synonymous with the Friday the 13th film series has never been filmed at the same lake twice. The locations of the eerie lake are as follows:

Friday the 13th (1980) – Sand Pond at Camp No-Be-Bo-Sco, Hardwick, New Jersey, USA.

Friday the 13th Part 2 (1981) – North Spectacle Pond, Kent, Connecticut.

Friday the 13th Part III (1982) – Valuzet Movie Ranch. The "lake" for this movie was specially created by the art department.

Friday the 13th: The Final Chapter (1984) – Zaca Lake, Santa Maria, California.

Friday the 13th: A New Beginning (1985) – no Jason Voorhees, so no Camp Crystal Lake! The movie was shot in California.

Jason Lives: Friday the 13th Part VI (1986) – Lake Rutledge at Camp Daniel Morgan in Hard Labor Creek State Park, Rutledge, Georgia, USA.

Friday the 13th Part VII: The New Blood (1988) – Byrnes Lake, Baldwin County, Alabama, USA.

Friday the 13th Part VIII: Jason Takes Manhattan (1989) – Britannia Beach, British Columbia, Canada.

Jason Goes to Hell: The Final Friday (1993) – The shots of the lake were archive footage from the Paramount library and were actually taken from the original *Friday the 13th* movie. The "lakeside" footage was filmed in Thousand Oaks, California, USA.

Jason X (2001) – Set mostly in space therefore there was no lake. However there was a sequence set within a holographic Camp Crystal Lake but this was shot in a studio using green screen and a digitally created lake and background.

Freddy vs. Jason (2003) – Buntzen Lake, Anmore, British Columbia, Canada.

Friday the 13th (2009) – Lake Bastrop, Bastrop County, Texas, USA – I was informed by director Marcus Nispel that three lakes were used to make Camp Crystal Lake in the film. He said, "The party house (Trent's Summer cabin) was not on a lake but the owner built a dam at a creek to create a sizeable pond where we shot smaller set-ups and tied it all in with Lake Bastrop. Altogether three lakes were pieced together to create Crystal Lake."

Ghostbusters (1984 - Directed by Ivan Reitman)

Dan Aykroyd has said that the original script was called *Ghost Mashers* and that himself, John Belushi and Eddie Murphy were set to play the three Ghostbusters.

Actor Bill Murray is rather unique in Hollywood in that he has no agent, no manager and no publicist. Instead he has a secret phone number that you call and leave a movie pitch after the tone if you want him to star in your movie.

Ghostbusters II (1989 – Directed by Ivan Reitman)

The twin babies that portrayed baby Oscar in the movie now both work together as martial arts instructors in San Diego. Aside from starring in the movie their other claim to fame is that their Uncle was the country music legend John Denver.

Ghostwatch (1992 – Directed by Lesley Manning)

This notorious BBC Television production was broadcast under the illusion that it was a real live TV show and not a cleverly scripted, orchestrated and pre-recorded piece of fictional drama. It was broadcast on Halloween night on BBC1 in 1992. It has never been re-shown by the BBC as a result of the psychological effects it had upon viewers. The show was listed in the British Medical Journal as inducing two cases of post-traumatic stress disorder in two 10-year-old boys. In a far more extreme case 18 year old Martin Denham, who had learning difficulties and a mental age of 13, committed suicide five days after watching the show by hanging himself from a tree with a length of plastic hosepipe. He had left a note in his back pocket that read, "Please don't worry – if there are ghosts I will be a ghost, and I will always be with you as a ghost."

A Good Marriage (2014 – Directed by Peter Askin)

Stephen King is said to have based the story featured in his 2010 book *Full Dark, No Stars* on serial killer Dennis Rader – also known as the BTK killer. Rader lived a seemingly normal life with his wife Paula and two children in Wichita, Kansas. He was a Cub Scout leader and had been elected president of the council at his local church. For 34 years of marriage his wife had no idea that her husband was the infamous BTK killer. Rader's grisly crimes had taken place between 1974 and 1991 and though he often taunted police with clues as to his identity he evaded capture until 2005. After years of silence he once again began to anonymously post information about his crimes to the media and police. Rader slipped up when he asked police in an anonymous letter if a floppy disk could be traced or not. The police lied to him and said it couldn't. Rader, taking the bait, sent a floppy disk to a TV channel in Wichita that the police traced back to the Christ Lutheran Church where he was president of the council. Police were able to determine that the last person to modify the disk was named *Dennis*. After his arrest Paula was granted an emergency divorce. When the self-penned Stephen King film adaptation was announced Rader's daughter Kerri broke the family's nine-year media silence on her father by condemning King for exploiting her father's ten victims and their families. She also said, "Great – now Stephen King is giving my father a big head. Thanks for that. That's the last thing my dad should get."

The Green Inferno (2013 – Directed by Eli Roth)

In order to achieve a high level of realism Roth ventured deep into the Amazon jungle to find a tribe who hadn't even seen a movie before. To give the remote Peruvian tribe he encountered an idea of what movies were he brought in a television and generator and showed them Ruggero Deodato's *Cannibal Holocaust*. According to Roth the tribe thought it was the funniest thing they had ever seen.

Gremlins (1984 – Directed by Joe Dante)

A few ideas were initially bandied around between the filmmakers on how they could achieve the special effects for the creatures. One of the more crazy suggestions was using monkeys! Joe Dante says that they went as far as putting a creature head onto a monkey and watching him chaotically cavort around the editing room. After observing the monkey, "Pooping on everything in terror," they wisely decided against the idea.

The fictional town of Kingston Falls was filmed on the Universal Studios backlot and is the same set that was used as Hill Valley in the *Back to the Future* movies.

Grindhouse (2007 – Directed by Robert Rodriguez, Quentin Tarantino, Rob Zombie, Edgar Wright, Eli Roth and Jason Eisener)

In order to get the cast and crew in the correct frame of mind for the project Tarantino and Rodriguez screened the movies *Torso* (1973) and Lucio Fulci's *Zombie* (1979) together with some old grindhouse movie trailers in between.

Actor Michael Parks, who has appeared in a number of Tarantino movies, was blacklisted by Hollywood in the 1970's and couldn't get any work for a number of years after making public comments about the producers wanting to make his TV show *Bronson* more violent. He claimed he didn't work for four years saying, "If you don't play their game, you don't work."

So far, two of the grindhouse trailers have gone on to become full length feature films. *Machete* (2010) and *Hobo with a Shotgun* (2011) were both directed by the original trailer director. Rob Zombie uploaded a five minute extended version of his *Werewolf Woman of the SS* trailer onto the internet in 2013 saying, "Boy, I wish we made this film... Maybe some day, but I doubt it." Eli Roth (*Thanksgiving* trailer) has said that he and Edgar Wright (*Don't* trailer) have discussed making feature length versions of their trailers and pairing the movies as a double bill in the same style as *Grindhouse* – possibly as *Grindhouse 2*. The poor box office reception of *Grindhouse* appears to be a contributing factor in Dimension Films not green-lighting the project.

Halloween (1978 – Directed by John Carpenter)

John Carpenter had originally sought both Christopher Lee and Peter Cushing for the role of Sam Loomis, both of whom declined.

As the film was shot in the spring in California, the production company had purchased a few bags of paper leaves which they painted in various autumnal colors and would liberally throw around before and during takes to make it look like autumn. After filming, the crew *and* the actors (this was low budget filmmaking after all!) would help gather up all the paper leaves from the streets in order for them to be re-used in other scenes.

In 2005 producer Moustapha Akkad, who was involved in every *Halloween* movie from the 1978 original through to *Halloween: Resurrection* in 2002, was killed at the Grand Hyatt hotel in Amman, Jordan. He had been inside the hotel with his 34 year-old daughter Rima Akkad Monla when a suicide bomber triggered an explosive device in the hotel's lobby where Moustapha and his daughter were attending a friend's wedding. His daughter was killed instantly whilst Moustapha held on for two days before succumbing to a severe heart attack as a result of the injuries he had sustained during the blast. Rob Zombie's 2007 *Halloween* remake would be dedicated to his memory.

Carpenter has said that interviewers often ask him what scares him and on one of the *Halloween* DVD commentaries he gives the following answer, "I think what scares me, scares every human on the planet. We're all aware of the forces of darkness, of evil, of loss, death... horror is the universal language."

Hannibal (2001 – Directed by Ridley Scott)

In 2013 Italian mobster Francesco Raccosta was murdered by Simone Pepe, a member of the Ndrangheta crime family in southern Italy. He was beaten with iron bars before being thrown into a sty where he was eaten alive by pigs. The horrific murder was said to be revenge for the killing of mafia boss Domenico Bonarrigo in 2012. Pepe boasted in police-taped phone calls that, "It was satisfying to hear him scream... nothing remained at all... wow, how a pig can eat!" Naturally the gruesome murder was compared to the film *Hannibal* in which Mason Verger is fed alive to his pigs by Hannibal Lecter.

Hellraiser (1987 – Directed by Clive Barker)

According to actress Ashley Lawrence (Kirsty) someone had committed suicide by gassing themselves in the garage of the house on Dollis Hill Lane in London where some of the movie was shot.

The scene in which Pinhead rises up behind Kirsty was achieved by having actor Doug Bradley stand on a seesaw-like contraption and be raised up by assistant director Selwyn Roberts. It somehow doesn't seem quite as scary when you picture Pinhead on a seesaw!

It is often mistakenly reported that four of the *Hellraiser* sequels began as totally unrelated spec scripts that had been optioned by the studio and, to save money, were rewritten to include reference to the cenobites and the whole *Hellraiser* mythology. It transpires this is only the case in two instances - *Hellraiser: Deader* (2005) and *Hellraiser: Hellworld* (2005).

Screenwriter Carl V. Dupre informed me that *Hellraiser: Hellseeker* (2002) was actually an original script. Dimension did own a spec script (strangely enough involving a computer virus, similar to *Hellraiser: Hellworld*) but they discarded this script and wrote an entirely new script from scratch. Also Scott Derrickson has told me that the script for *Hellraiser: Inferno* was specifically written as a *Hellrasiser* screenplay by himself and Paul Harris Boardman. Doug Bradley (Pinhead) gives a conflicting account in his book *Behind the Mask of the Horror Actor* and claims it was based on a pre-existing script. I think I choose to believe the writers!

Hellraiser: Deader (2005) started out as a script by Neal Marshall Stevens simply called *Deader* that ended up in the hands of Bob Weinstein at Dimension Films who loved it and optioned it within days of reading it. The script was then developed over an eighteen-month period in its pre-*Hellraiser* form but the project was ultimately dropped. A few months went by before Stevens was contacted to see if he would be interested in re-writing *Deader* as a *Hellraiser* movie. He opted to pass but as the studio owned the screenplay they were free to do as they wished. Screenwriter Tim Day (who had also worked on the *Hellseeker* script) was brought in to adapt it – changing, amongst other things, the location from New York City to Bucharest.

Hellraiser: Hellworld (2005) was adapted from a twenty-page script treatment called *Dark Can't Breathe* by Joel Session.

The eighth *Hellraiser* sequel, *Hellraiser: Revelations* (2011), was rushed into production in order for Dimension Films to retain the rights to the franchise. Despite the rapidity of the production an original screenplay was written. Doug Bradley has said that part of his decision to not return to the role of Pinhead (which he had portrayed in every film since the original) was based on the rushed nature of the project.

Henry: Portrait of a Serial Killer (1986 – Directed by John McNaughton)

It took over ten years for the British Board of Film Classification to approve the uncut version of the movie. They had previously cut one minute and fifty three seconds from it. James Ferman of the BBFC was criticized for re-editing the film in such a way that it changed the fundamental meaning of the filmmaker's original vision.

Despite being filmed in 1985 the film didn't get released until 1990 but this was only partly due to the violent nature of the film. Another reason offered by director McNaughton is that the producers were underwhelmed by the movie and wanted to shelf it. In 1989 film director Chuck Parello was working for the producers when he viewed a copy and urged them to release it. Parello would go on to direct the 1996 sequel *Henry II: Portrait of a Serial Killer.*

The film was Michael Rooker's (Henry) debut feature film and he was said to have remained in character for most of the month-long shoot. According to costume designer Patricia Hart (who drove with Rooker to the set) she sometimes couldn't distinguish if she was talking with Michael or Henry.

The Hills Have Eyes Part II (1984 – Directed by Wes Craven)

Wes Craven claims that the studio pulled the plug on the movie after only two thirds of it were shot, owing to budget concerns. After the success of Craven's *A Nightmare on Elm Street* they reevaluated the box office potential for the film and asked Craven to return to complete it but only using what he had already shot. In order to pad out the running time Craven resorted to using lengthy flashbacks, taking footage from the first film – even going to the ridiculous length of giving the dog his own flashback scene! The resulting film was widely panned by critics and was ultimately disowned by Craven.

The Innkeepers (2011 – Directed by Ti West)

Unlike The Overlook Hotel in *The Shining,* the Yankee Pedlar Inn in *The Innkeepers* is a real hotel located in Torrington, Connecticut. The hotel is supposedly haunted by the hotel's original owners, Frank and Alice Conley. The movie was entirely filmed inside the real Yankee Pedlar Inn over 17 days and the cast and crew all lived there together for the duration of the shoot. During shooting the cast and crew experienced a fair amount of strange phenomena including lights switching on and off, doors swinging open by themselves, TV's turning themselves on and phones ringing with no-one on the other end. Ti West said the strangest thing that happened was choosing a particular room (the honeymoon suite) to feature as the haunted room in the movie. West maintains that he selected it for purely technical reasons (it was the end of a hallway making it ideal for a dolly shot). It turned out that the honeymoon suite was the hotel's most haunted room.

Whilst Ti West was shooting *The House of the Devil* (2009) he stayed at the Yankee Pedlar Inn - because it was cheap and near to the location. His stay there inspired him to write *The Innkeepers* script.

Interview with the Vampire: The Vampire Chronicles (1994 – Directed by Neil Jordan)

Author Anne Rice had openly disapproved of the casting of Tom Cruise as the Vampire Lestat but having been sent a copy of the finished film by producer David Geffen she bought a two-page ad in Variety and The New York Times to declare her love for the movie and highly praised Cruise's performance. No equivalent letter was forthcoming for the sequel, *Queen of the Damned* - Rice has, instead, publically said, "I didn't care for the movie of *The Queen of the Damned* at all."

River Phoenix had initially been cast in the role of the "interviewer" Daniel Malloy but on account of his untimely death in 1993 from a drug overdose Christian Slater was brought in to replace him. Slater, feeling awkward to be, "Stepping into that kind of scenario," donated his entire salary to River Phoenix's charities.

Whilst Brad Pitt was living in London during shooting, the house that he occupied once belonged to Peter Cushing - Cushing was of course rather well known for playing Dracula's nemesis Abraham Van Helsing in the Hammer Horror movies. After an interview with Chris Heath for Empire magazine (conducted whilst Pitt was in London shooting *Interview with the Vampire*), Pitt got up from the table at a pie shop in Notting Hill, where they had chatted, and went to unlock his bicycle to return to Cushing's old house. He told Heath that he has numerous bicycles locked up all over the world in various locations, "When I leave a place I find a good hiding place and lock it up... I have two in Amsterdam, a bike in Canada, a bike in Oregon, New York, New Orleans and Vegas."

The Island of Dr. Moreau (1996 – Directed by John Frankenheimer)

Director Richard Stanley (*Hardware* and *Dust Devil*) had spent years developing his dream project of H.G. Wells' *The Island of Dr. Moreau* only to end up being fired after just three days shooting and replaced with *Birdman of Alcatraz* director John Frankenheimer. It has been suggested that star Val Kilmer had something to do with Stanley's premature departure.

Though banned from returning to the set, Stanley donned a dog creature costume to witness first hand the ensuing mayhem of the chaotic production. He claimed it actually cheered him up somewhat to observe how much worse the production was without him. The movie went wildly over schedule and over budget and the resulting film was very badly received, garnering six Razzie Award nominations (with one win for Marlon Brando as Worst Actor).

Clearly Kilmer and Frankenheimer had also clashed on the troubled set resulting in Frankenheimer allegedly ending the last ever take of shooting with, "Cut. Now get that bastard off my set." Frankenheimer was also quoted in interviews as saying, "There are two things I will never do in my life. I will never climb Mount Everest, and I will never work with Val Kilmer again."

It (1990 – Directed by Tommy Lee Wallace)

Actors John Ritter and Jonathan Brandis both tragically died in 2003 within a month of each other. Ritter died suddenly from an aortic dissection while Brandis committed suicide by hanging himself.

Tim Curry (Pennywise) was born in Warrington, England – the same town that I'm from! A slightly self-indulgent bit of trivia, sorry!

Jason X (2001 – Directed by James Isaac)

On 23rd March 2015, a man was attacked in his own home in Manchester, England by three men, one of whom wielded a machete and wore a Jason X style Uber Jason mask. Thankfully the man survived the seemingly motiveless attack.

Jaws (1975 – Directed by Steven Spielberg)

Jaws is loosely based on a series of shark attacks that took place along the coast of New Jersey in the summer of 1916. Between July 1st and July 12th four people were killed and one was badly injured when an undetermined species of shark made its way up the coast during a heat wave. The International Shark Attack File lists the victims as being killed by a great white shark and indeed a juvenile great white was caught in the area a few days after the final attack. Others believe it could have been a bull shark. The story of the attacks served as more direct source material in the 2005 TV movie *12 Days of Terror* directed by Jack Sholder (*A Nightmare on Elm Street Part 2: Freddy's Revenge, The Hidden*).

According to Carl Gottlieb in his book *The Jaws Log,* during the early stages of development the producers Richard D. Zanuck and David Brown assumed that they would be able to hire somebody to actually train a great white shark to perform in the film.

Gottlieb also recounts in *The Jaws Log* having dinner with the police chief of Edgartown on Martha's Vineyard (where the movie was filmed) with whom he broached the subject of the Chappaquiddick Incident (the Ted Kennedy car crash that killed passenger Mary Jo Kopechne). The chief's demeanor shifted to anger as he informed them how all the evidence relating to the case went missing from the official police files. As a result of chronicling the dinner table conversation in his book, Gottlieb was contacted by unnamed persons in the Republican camp who wanted more information. He told them that all he knew was printed in the book and subsequently a new inquiry was launched which simply concluded that the files were, indeed, missing.

In recent years there have been countless direct-to-video *Jaws* rip-offs usually featuring a dreadfully rendered computer-generated shark and a ridiculous title. They include *Malibu Shark Attack* (2009), *Swamp Shark* (2011), *Shark in Venice* (2008), *2-Headed Shark Attack* (2012), *Jersey Shore Shark Attack* (2012), *Avalanche Sharks* (2013), *Dinoshark* (2010), *Snow Shark* (2011), *Sharktopus* (2010), *Sharktopus vs. Pteracuda* (2014), *Super Shark* (2011), *Sand Sharks* (2011), *Jurassic Shark* (2012), *Ghost Shark* (2013) *Ghost Shark 2: Urban Jaws* (2015) *Piranha Sharks* (2014), *Mega Shark vs. Giant Octopus* (2009) *Mega Shark vs. Crocosaurus* (2010), *Mega Shark vs. Mecha Shark* (2014), *Sharknado* (2013), *Sharknado 2: The Second One* (2014), *Sharknado 3: Oh Hell No!* (2015) and the brilliantly named *Raiders of the Lost Shark* (2014).

Director Bryan Singer (*The Usual Suspects*, *X-Men*) is such a big fan of the film that he named his production company, Bad Hat Harry Productions, after a line in the film – from the scene where Chief Brody is teased for being afraid of the water and retorts with, "That's some bad hat, Harry."

Jaws 2 (1978 – Directed by Jeannot Szwarc)

Because there wasn't really an appropriate French translation for the word 'jaws' the original movie was renamed *Les Dents De La Mer* (translated as 'The Teeth of the Sea') in France. This posed a problem for the sequel because adding a '2' to *Les Dents De La Mer* resulted in it, phonetically, sounding like Les Dents De La Merde (mer and deux) – the English translation of which is 'The Teeth of the Shit'. To avoid this ridiculous (though rather amusing) title it had to be changed to *Les Dents de la mer 2ème partie* (*Part* 2).

Jaws: The Revenge (1987 – Directed by Joseph Sargent)

Often considered to be one of the worst films ever made *Jaws: The Revenge* was nominated for seven Razzie Awards (winning one for Worst Visual Effects). Sir Michael Caine missed receiving his Best Supporting Actor Oscar for *Hannah and Her Sisters* (1986) as a result of working on the movie. When asked if he had ever seen it Caine replied, "I have never seen it, but by all accounts it is terrible. However, I have seen the house that it built, and it is terrific."

Judith Barsi, the actress who played Ellen Brody's granddaughter, Thea, was murdered in 1988 by her father, József. She had suffered years of physical and mental abuse at the hands of her abusive dad. On the evening of July 25th he shot Judith in the head whilst she was sleeping before shooting his wife Maria in their home in Los Angeles. Two days later he poured gasoline onto their bodies and set them alight before entering the garage and shooting himself in the head with a .32 caliber pistol. Disturbingly during the two days he was alone with the bodies, József spoke to Judith's agent over the phone, telling her he intended to move out for good but needed some time to, "Say goodbye to my little girl."

Jeepers Creepers (2001 – Directed by Victor Salva)

The opening scenes of the film bear an uncanny resemblance to an episode of the TV show *Unsolved Mysteries* that focused on the case of Dennis DePue – a Michigan resident who murdered his wife and dumped her body behind an abandoned schoolhouse. A couple, Ray and Marie Thornton, were driving by when they witnesses DePue with a bloody sheet acting suspiciously, and a few minutes later they found themselves being pursued by him in his vehicle. After taking a turning off the road the couple decided to go back to the schoolhouse to investigate and discovered the bloody sheet partially stuffed into an animal hole. DePue was only tracked down once the *Unsolved Mysteries* episode aired but he committed suicide before the police could capture him.

Kill List (2011 – Directed by Ben Wheatley)

Even though Wheatley's film has often been compared to such movies as *The Wicker Man* and *The Blair Witch Project,* the director claims it was inspired by his childhood nightmares, "Things like cults in the woods and the tunnels is all stuff I've had as a recurring nightmare since I was very little. I used to live near the woods."

Lake Placid (1999 – Directed by Steve Miner)

Special effects guru Stan Winston had originally wanted to create small animatronic crocodiles for the final shot of the movie but director Steve Miner thought it was going to be too complicated and expensive. Winston didn't believe they would be able to get the shot with real baby crocs.

Undeterred by Winston's advice, Miner brought in some baby caiman's and released them into the water, achieving the perfect shot in the very first take.

Leatherface: The Texas Chainsaw Massacre III (1990 – Directed by Jeff Burr)

The executives at New Line Cinema originally wanted Peter Jackson to direct the movie but he declined. Years later they would eventually get to work with him on *The Lord of the Rings* and *The Hobbit* films.

The theatrical poster for the film misspelt two of the actor's names - Ken Foree (Benny) was spelt as Ken Force and Toni Hudson (Sara) was spelt as Tom Hudson. For home video releases of the film, Foree's name has been corrected but Toni Hudson remains as Tom Hudson!

Legacy of Thorn (2014 – Directed by Mj Dixon)

The film was shot in an abandoned school in Oldham, England, where the cast and crew stayed for the duration of the shoot. The unsettling nature of the location was further heightened when the actors began to notice an old kettle mysteriously move from room to room. Actor Nathan Head recalled, "It just kept appearing in odd places, when nobody was there that could have moved it. It firstly appeared on the main staircase and then a short time later in the middle of a hallway." The cast and crew would continue to find the kettle in different locations and every time there was nobody around that could have possibly moved it! That's one creepy kettle!

The Lost Boys (1987 – Directed by Joel Schumacher)

Before the sequels *Lost Boys: The Tribe* (2008) and *Lost Boys: The Thirst* (2010) were made it had always been the intention for the sequel to be *The Lost Girls*. Despite a script being written the project never got off the ground.

In 2001 a washed up Corey Haim (Sam) was so broke that he had resorted to selling clumps of his hair and an extracted (decayed) tooth on eBay. The tooth was almost sold, for just $150, but the listing was pulled in line with eBay's policy on the sale of body parts. Having struggled with drug addiction for most of his life Haim sadly died on March 10th, 2010, at the age of 38. Initially it was speculated it had been from a heroin overdose but his cause of death was later confirmed as pneumonia; the toxicology report having shown no evidence of any significant contributing factor.

Maximum Overdrive (1986 – Directed by Stephen King)

Whilst shooting the scene in which the lawnmower chases Deke through the suburbs, the radio-controlled prop lawnmower went out of control for real and hit a block of wood that was supporting a camera, causing wood splinters to shoot out everywhere. Unfortunately the director of photography, Armando Nannuzzi, was injured in the incident and lost his right eye. He would later go on to sue Stephen King in 1987 for $18 million in damages. The suit was settled out of court.

Stephen King admits to being so, "Coked out of his mind," during shooting that he often didn't know what he was doing.

The Mirror (2014 – Directed by Ed Boase)

Director Ed Boase was inspired to write the movie after hearing about a haunted mirror that had been put up for sale on eBay by two London flat mates, Sotiris Charalambous and Joseph Birch. Having acquired the antique mirror from a nearby skip, the pair began to experience unexplainable phenomena in their flat. They were plagued by terrible nightmares and incurred bodily injuries as they slept. Objects moved around the flat by themselves and they witnessed haunting images within the mirror itself. Things got so bad that one of the pair was given antidepressants; the other was taken to hospital after experiencing crippling pains in his legs. They theorized that someone had likely been murdered in front of the mirror - Charalambous claimed to have photographed a small man with a hood in the mirror, hacking downwards with a spike or knife.

Their listing on eBay chronicled their supernatural ordeal and they stated that they wished for the mirror to be purchased by somebody with paranormal experience who, "Knows what they are getting themselves in for." Eventually a collector of occult paraphernalia from Germany bought the cursed mirror.

I was informed by the film's director, Ed Boase, that when the mirror was shipped to Germany, a worker at the shipping company was hospitalized after badly cutting his hand open whilst handling the crate that housed the mysterious mirror.

Mother's Day (1980 – Directed by Charles Kaufman)

It is often said that a murder occurred in the house that was used during the filming of the movie in Newton, New Jersey. Supposedly it happened 15 years before the filmmakers began making the movie. Some people have even claimed that a dead body was found in the house whilst they were there. However, these stories appear to be fabricated. I contacted a couple of the production crew for their take on the story:

Production designer Susan Lisbeth Kaufman told me, "No, there were no bodies found in the house during our time there. By the condition we found the house in I would imagine we were the first to enter in many, many years. I believe there were some dead animals! The place was a disaster that we not only had to clean out but also had to exterminate." Rex Piano, the assistant art director said, "I never heard the rumor of someone being murdered there. As I recall, the owner of the home died in it and when we went to prep the house for filming there was at least two feet deep of old magazines in various rooms."

The film was shot at the same time as *Friday the 13th* (1980) and even features an almost identical shot of a vehicle driving along Millbrook road in Hardwick Township, New Jersey.

Incredibly the film wasn't released for home video distribution in the UK until January 2015, having initially been rejected for a theatrical release way back in 1980.

My Name Is Bruce (2007 – Directed by Bruce Campbell)

The nearest town to the production was Jacksonville, Oregon, which Bruce Campbell said would have been a perfect location for the film but because the annual Britt Music Festival was in town at the same time they wanted to shoot, Campbell opted to build a small town set on his own property near Medford, Oregon.

The film contained many performances from actors involved in the *Evil Dead* films including Ellen Sandweiss (Cheryl from *The Evil Dead*), Ted Raimi (possessed Henrietta from *Evil Dead II*), Dan Hicks (Jake from *Evil Dead II*) and Timothy Patrick Quill (blacksmith from *Army of Darkness*). The film also featured performances from Bruce's brother Mike and his nephew Colin Campbell.

A Nightmare on Elm Street (1984 – Directed by Wes Craven)

Wes Craven has said that the inspiration for the story came from real-life cases of people dying in their sleep. He read about the incidents in the LA Times that reported the deaths of Khmer refuges who were complaining of disturbing nightmares spurned by their experiences of war in Cambodia. Just like in the movie they were terrified of going to sleep and ultimately ended up dying in the midst of their nightmares.

Johnny Depp went along to the auditions for the movie with his friend Jackie Earle Haley, and even though it was Haley who was auditioning for the role of Glen, Wes Craven spotted Depp and asked him to audition. Depp was ultimately cast as Glen but Jackie Earle Haley would go on to star as Freddy Krueger himself in the 2010 remake of *A Nightmare on Elm Street*.

In the early 2000s *Henry Portrait of a Serial Killer* director John McNaughton was in talks to direct a prequel to *A Nightmare on Elm Street* addressing the backstory of Freddy Krueger. He naturally surmised that if Freddy ended up in Hell then that would be where he started. The idea of making a movie set in Hell excited McNaughton but sadly didn't impress the executives at New Line Cinema - owing to the box office failure of the Adam Sandler comedy *Little Nicky* that featured many scenes in Hell. McNaughton said, "New Line didn't want to go back to Hell. So I basically told them to go to Hell!"

A prequel had been made before, though not as a feature film. In 1988 *The Texas Chain Saw Massacre* director Tobe Hooper filmed an episode of the *Freddy's Nightmares* TV show (starring Robert Englund as Freddy Krueger) called *No More Mr. Nice Guy* that focused on Freddy's acquittal and subsequent murder at the hands of his victim's parents. The episode was the pilot for a series that would run for two seasons and contain episodes directed by such people as Tom McLoughlin (*Jason Lives: Friday the 13th Part VI*), Mick Garris (*Psycho IV: The Beginning*), Ken Wiederhorn (*Return of the Living Dead II*), Dwight H. Little (*Halloween 4: The Return of Michael Myers*) as well as Robert Englund himself (who directed two episodes).

<u>Night of the Living Dead (1968 – Directed by George A. Romero)</u>

As a result of the film's original distributor neglecting to put a copyright indication on the film's prints, the movie had no copyright and was considered to be in the public domain. As a result of this there are almost 200 distributors who have released the film for home video.

Aside from the official George A. Romero sequels there have been numerous films produced utilizing a variation of the *Night of the Living Dead* title including: *Flight of the Living Dead* (2007), *Knight of the Living Dead* (2005), *Night of the Living Dorks* (2004), *Raiders of the Living Dead* (1986), *Night of the Living Heads* (2010), *Night of the Living Deb* (2015), *Night of the Living Babes* (1987), *Nightmare of the Living Dead* (1998), *Hood of the Living Dead* (2005), *Nerd of the Living Dead* (2011), *Night of the Living Lasagna* (2006) and there is a film listed as being in development on IMDb called *Night of the Living Dong*. I'm not saying anything... but I think I want to see it!

There are also a huge number of films more directly using Romero's original story and purporting to be remakes or reimagining's or rehashes or rip-offs! They include: *Night of the Living Dead* (1990), *Another Night of the Living Dead* (2011), *Night of the Living Dead 3D* (2006), *Night of the Living Dead 3D: Re-Animation* (2012), *Night of the Living Dead: Origins 3D* (2015), *Night of the Living Dead: Resurrection* (2012), *Night of the Living Dead* (2014), *Night of the Living Dead: Reanimated* (2009), *Night of the Living 3D Dead* (2013), *Night of the Living Dead: Genesis* (2015), *Night of the*

Living Dead: Contagion (2015), *Night of the Living Dead: Rebirth* (2015) as well as the documentary film *Birth of the Living Dead* (2013). And let us not forget the bizarrely titled *Night of the Day of the Dawn of the Son of the Bride of the Return of the Terror* (1991) – seriously!

Nosferatu (1922 – Directed by F.W. Murnau)

This seminal and iconic German Expressionist horror film was very nearly completely wiped from existence when Bram Stoker's widow, Florence, successfully sued the filmmakers for copyright infringement, claiming it was a direct and unauthorized adaptation of *Dracula*. The court ordered that all existing copies of the film be destroyed. Thankfully one copy survived that had already been shipped overseas. *Phew!*

The film remained banned in Sweden until 1972 due to its excessive horror. It's a good job the one surviving print hadn't been sent there!

Max Schreck's (Count Orlok) surname in Germany literally means 'fright'. And it's not even a stage name!

Even though Murnau's *Nosferatu* just escaped from being a 'lost film' many of his other films are now considered to be lost, including an unauthorized adaption of Robert Louis Stevenson's *Strange Case of Dr. Jekyll and Mr. Hyde* called *The Head of Janus* (1920), starring Bela Lugosi.

The Omen (1976 – Directed by Richard Donner)

One of the most famous films associated with a film-curse and for good reason too! Here are just a few examples of the purported curse:

On the way to the location, star Gregory Peck's airplane was struck by lighting, as was screenwriter's David Seltzner's different flight.

A plane that had been hired for aerial filming, but was chartered to a different client at the last minute, crashed – killing everyone on board.

Both a hotel and a restaurant were bombed by the IRA that the cast and crew were using.

There was a head-on car crash involving the production crew on the first day of filming.

Strangest of all has to be the car crash that took place on Friday the 13th of August 1976. John Richardson, who had created the special effects for the decapitation scene in *The Omen* was involved in a collision that decapitated his assistant, Liz Moore. When Richardson clambered out of the wreckage he looked up to see a road sign that chillingly read, '*Ommen: 66.6 km*'. With all these real-life horrific events it's amazing that anyone ever signed on for the sequels or remake!

Paranormal Activity (2007 – Directed by Oren Peli)

When Steven Spielberg watched an early cut of the movie at night he was so scared that he turned it off and watched the rest of the film the next day. When he went back to his bedroom to view the rest of the movie, his bedroom door had inexplicably locked itself shut from the inside and a locksmith had to be called in. Apparently a saw had to be used to cut the door open because the locksmith couldn't open it!

Parents (1989 – Directed by Bob Balaban)

Actor Randy Quaid, who starred in this strange horror comedy (known as *Daddy is a Cannibal* in Germany!), has in recent times been absent from the filmmaking world. His last listed credit is a film called *Star Whackers* (2011), a documentary in which Quaid claims that an elite group in Hollywood are out to kill him and his wife, Evi. He believes that actors such as Heath Ledger, David Carradine and Chris Penn have all been killed by the evil group. He currently resides in Canada with his wife and they are presently unable to return to the United States as they are wanted for a number of offences including failure to pay a substantial hotel bill and for vandalizing their former home. In May 2015 Randy Quaid was finally discovered to be living above a garage in small apartment in Montreal. After he was arrested his neighbor, Ivan Mulkeen, said on Twitter that he had no idea the movie star was living next door to him.

Plan 9 From Outer Space (1959 - Directed by Edward D. Wood Jr.)

The studio building (then called Quality Studios) where Ed Wood shot a lot of the scenes for the movie recently went up for sale on LoopNet. It is advertised on their website as *Ed Wood's Soundstage*. It is said that Jimi Hendrix, The Doors and Guns N' Roses had all used the building as a rehearsal room over the years.

Twenty years after Ed Wood's death his previously unfilmed script entitled *I Woke Up Early The Day I Died* (1998) was produced and featured a star-studded cast including, Billy Zane, Ron Perlman, Christina Ricci, Andrew McCarthy, Tippi Hedren, John Ritter, Sandra Bernhard, Karen Black, Eartha Kitt as well *Plan 9 From Outer Space* actors Conrad Brooks and Vampira in her last feature film appearance.

Poltergeist (1982 – Directed by Tobe Hooper)

There has been a lot of confusion over who actually directed the film with some people arguing that it was predominately directed by writer and producer Steven Spielberg. Tobe Hooper has said that the rumors began when the L.A. Times arrived on set whilst Spielberg was directing some second-unit material and they assumed Spielberg had taken over. Hooper maintains that he directed the movie but Spielberg's open letter to Hooper (printed in The Hollywood Reporter) does seem to suggest that Spielberg was given quite a, "Wide berth for creative involvement." Spielberg diplomatically said that the press misunderstood their, "Rather unique creative relationship," and praised Hooper for performing responsibly and professionally and delivering the goods. Without having been present for the duration of the shoot it's very difficult to determine the truth of the matter but it's probably best concluded by saying both Spielberg and Hooper *made* the film together.

Along with *The Omen* and *The Exorcist*, *Poltergeist* is often associated with having a curse, owing to the deaths of four of the actors within six years of each other. The rumored curse was often said to have manifested as a consequence of the prop department using real skeletons (apparently they were cheaper than plastic ones!). The most shocking death was arguably Dominique Dunne who played the eldest daughter, Dana. She was killed by her boyfriend, John Thomas Sweeney just months after the film's release. Sweeney had strangled her after she had broken up with him a few weeks earlier, causing her to fall into a coma and dying five days later - her co-star, 12 year old Heather O'Rourke (Carol Anne), would be buried in the same cemetery as Dunne (Westwood Village Memorial Park) six years later after a cardiac arrest caused by septic shock. Incredibly Sweeney was only charged with voluntary manslaughter (killing in the "heat of passion") and only served three years and seven months of his six and a half year sentence.

When he was released he worked as a sous chef in a restaurant in Santa Monica where Dominique's mother and her brother Griffin (*An American Werewolf in London* star, Griffin Dunne) began handing out flyers stating that the food they were eating was cooked by the man who killed Dominique Dunne. In the 1990's Dominique's father, Dominick, was contacted by a doctor in Florida who was worried that his daughter might have just become engaged to John Sweeney, which it turned out was indeed the case. Griffin Dunne called the daughter to persuade her to call the engagement off but Sweeney accused the Dunnes of harassing him and abruptly changed his name and disappeared. Unperturbed the Dunnes hired a private investigator to track him down and were informed he had moved to the Pacific Northwest and changed his named to John Maura. Eventually

Dominick Dunne decided that he no longer wanted to waste his life away pursuing Sweeney and the investigations were called off.

Primeval (2007 – Directed by Michael Katleman)

The real crocodile, named Gustave, which the film is based on, is perhaps not such as prolific a killer as depicted in the film. Travel writer Richard Grant met Patrice Faye (a Frenchman who has studied Gustave for many years in Burundi and who actually gave the croc its name) who immediately defended the killer croc when asked about his alleged 300 plus killings, "No, no, no, this is what they write but it is not true. I have investigated every case for eleven years, and Gustave he has killed only sixty people, maybe even less." Faye had originally hunted the giant crocodile (estimated to be over a hundred years old, weighing a ton and measuring over 18 feet) and had even shot at him a few times but after he got a really good look at him one day he decided that he wanted to save and protect the large beast. Faye said, "I see this magnificent prehistoric creature, the last of the really big crocodiles. I put the rifle down. I cannot kill him." Gustave was never captured and has since vanished, presumed dead – but who knows?

Psycho (1960 – Directed by Alfred Hitchcock)

Myra Jones was an actress who was Janet Leigh's stand-in for Marion Crane on *Psycho*. In 1988 she was raped and murdered by her neighbor, Kenneth Dean Hunt – a man who was said to have been obsessed with the film as well as Janet Leigh. It is believed that he intended to kill Janet Leigh's body double for the shower sequence, Marli Renfro, and for many years it was commonly thought that he had indeed murdered Renfro instead of Jones. Perhaps Hunt was unclear on the difference between a stand-in (used off-screen for technical reasons/lighting set-ups) and a body double (used on-screen to perform scenes an actor can't or won't do). Robert Graysmith (author of *Zodiac*) wrote a book trying to make sense of the whole mess called *The Girl in Alfred Hitchcock's Shower*.

Film director Steven Soderbergh edited together the original *Psycho* film with Gus Van Sant's shot-by-shot color remake, creating a mash-up of both films entitled *Psychos*. The shower sequence is a particular highlight as Soderbergh layers the two versions over each other creating quite a visually stimulating experience.

The description of Norman Bates in Robert Bloch's original *Psycho* novel differs quite considerably from how the character would go on to be portrayed in the movies. Bloch states that Norman had a plump face, rimless glasses and thinning sandy hair.

Psycho II (1983 – Directed by Richard Franklin)

Anthony Perkins had originally declined to return in the role of Norman Bates but when he heard they were going to go ahead without him (with Christopher Walken as Norman Bates) he agreed to star in the film.

Alfred Hitchcock makes a posthumous cameo appearance in the movie in the form of a shadow of his famous silhouette – it's on the wall in Norma Bates' room when Norman and Mary enter the room before turning on the lights.

Queen of the Damned (2002 – Directed by Michael Rymer)

Korn frontman Jonathan Davis wrote and performed the songs for Lestat's band but contractual differences meant that he couldn't appear on the film's soundtrack album, so the songs were re-recorded with other singers including David Draiman of Disturbed, Chester Bennington of Linkin Park and Marilyn Manson.

Aaliyah, who played the ancient vampire Queen Akasha, was killed in a plane crash shortly after principle photography on the film. The crash was said to have been caused by overloading the small plane that went down very shortly after take off, killing everyone on board. A month before her death she had given an interview with Die Zeit (a weekly German newspaper), in which she eerily recounted a recurring dream that foretold her untimely death. She said the dream featured her in the dark, feeling scared and someone was following her, "Then, suddenly, I lift off. Far away. How do I feel? As if I am swimming in the air. Free. Nobody can reach me. Nobody can touch me."

Stuart Townsend (the Vampire Lestat) had been originally hired to play Aragorn in the *Lord of the Rings* trilogy but was fired the day before filming began. No formal statement from New Line was ever issued, though it has often been suggested that the actor looked too young for the role. Other sources suggest the studio wanted a more recognizable actor in the role.

On December the 11th, 2002, 22-year-old Allan Menzies brutally killed his friend Thomas McKendrick and drank his blood at his home in West Lothian, Scotland. Menzies was obsessed with the *Queen of the Damned* film and had watched it over a hundred times. He claimed that Aaliyah's vampire character had visited him and told him he would be rewarded with immortality if he killed someone. During his trial Menzies told the court, "If you don't murder somebody you couldn't become a vampire." Shortly after being jailed for life, Menzies was found dead in his prison cell having hanged himself.

Re-Animator (1985 – Directed by Stuart Gordon)

The first corpse to be re-animated in the movie is portrayed by Peter Kent, who has been Arnold Schwarzenegger's stunt double in 14 of his movies. Kent was involved in a near-fatal motorcycle accident in the early 80's and his reconstructive surgery left him with features that closely resembled those of Schwarzenegger.

In 2011 Stuart Gordon wrote, produced and directed a stage production of the film called *Re-Animator: The Musical*. The production has been staged a number of times in various locations and has won several awards. Note: Avoid sitting on the front three rows of the theater if you don't wish to be covered in fake blood!

The Rocky Horror Picture Show (1975 – Directed by Jim Sharman)

Oakley Court was the rather grand and gothic house in Berkshire, England, used as the main location for the film, both inside and out. It has been used in many other horror movies including *The Curse of Frankenstein* (1957), *Dracula* (1974), *The Evil of Frankenstein* (1964), *Monster of Terror* (1965), *The Reptile* (1966), *The Plague of the Zombies* (1966), *And Now the Screaming Starts!* (1973), *The Brides of Dracula* (1960), *The Old Dark House* (1963), *Witchcraft* (1964), *Nightmare* (1964), Vampyres (1974) and *The House in Nightmare Park* (1973).

The follow-up film to *The Rocky Horror Picture Show* was the critical and financial failure *Shock Treatment* (1981). Despite its negative reputation it has recently gone on to be staged at the King's Head Theatre in London. Unlike the movie it seems to have been greeted with positive reviews from both critics and audiences.

A third movie was written by Richard O'Brien in the late 80's/early 90's called *Revenge of the Old Queen* and featured Riff Raff being sent back to Earth from the planet of Transsexual by Frank 'N' Furter's mother to find her son. In a rather postmodern way the film *The Rocky Horror Picture Show* exists within the narrative and the characters make reference to it - believing that it was based on a true story. It was in development at Fox but never went into production and currently looks like it will never be made. Then again, I don't think anyone foresaw *Shock Treatment* being produced for the London stage!

Rosemary's Baby (1968 – Directed by Roman Polanski)

John Lennon was a resident of the Dakota apartment building in New York City where *Rosemary's Baby* was filmed. On December 8th, 1980, Mark David Chapman shot and killed Lennon as he exited the building. Chillingly six hours before his death Lennon had autographed a copy of his *Double Fantasy* album for his future murderer.

A year after the release of the film, Roman Polanski's pregnant wife (actress Sharon Tate) was murdered by members of the Manson Family in the Hollywood Hills. Strangely enough The Manson Family nicknamed their murder spree *Helter Skelter*, after The Beatles song, leading some people to believe Tate's and Lennon's murders were somehow connected.

There was a sequel made as a TV movie called *Look What's Happened to Rosemary's Baby* (1976) that focused on the life of Rosemary's son, Adrian, from a young boy to an adult. The only star from the original movie was Ruth Gordon who reprised her Oscar winning role as Minnie Castevet.

Producer William Castle believed the film to be cursed after falling ill from kidney failure. He underwent a number of surgeries and is alleged to have said at one point during his treatment, "Rosemary, for God's sake drop that knife."

Shark! (1969 – Directed by Samuel Fuller)

Though not quite a horror movie, this Troma Entertainment film is quite notable for its horrific shark attack that took place whilst shooting the movie on location in Mexico. Stunt performer Jose Marco was killed on camera by a bull shark whilst shooting footage involving a sedated tiger shark. The rogue shark swam through a protective net where the underwater team were shooting the Burt Reynolds movie and viciously attacked the 32-year-old performer – who died on the way to hospital. In a rather bad taste move the producers used his death to promote the movie – they changed the title from *Caine* (the name of Burt Reynolds' character) to *Shark!* They even had an illustration of a man being attacked by a shark on the poster together with the tag line, "Will rip you apart". Making matters even worse, the film was re-released by Legacy Entertainment in 2003 under the new title of *Man-Eater*.

The Shining (1980 – Directed by Stanley Kubrick)

Now regarded as a classic horror film, the film received some negative reviews at the time of release. Stanley Kubrick was even nominated for a Golden Raspberry Award for Worst Director! Thankfully he lost out to Robert Greenwald for *Xanadu*.

As featured in the documentary feature film *Room 237* there are some bizarre theories about the true meaning of Kubrick's film. Some believe it to be about the genocide of the Native Americans whilst others think it's about the Holocaust. Another theory by Jay Weidner is that Kubrick was hiding

75

clues throughout the film that suggested he was involved with faking the Apollo 11 moon landing footage. The evidence he puts forward is quite compelling and includes: Danny wearing an Apollo 11 knitted jumper; Kubrick changing the room number from the book's original 217 to 237 (the average distance to the moon is 237,000 miles); the phrase that Jack repeatedly types out, 'All work and no play makes Jack a dull boy' contains a reference to Apollo 11 in the word 'All'; the hexagonal carpet pattern resembles the Apollo 11 launching pads; the hotel manager has an eagle on his windowsill (the nickname for the Apollo 11 lunar module was *The Eagle*). Adding to his theory is the fact that Kubrick made *2001: A Space Odyssey* (1968), which shows astronauts on the surface of the moon.

The Silence of the Lambs (1990 – Directed by Jonathan Demme)

Before Anthony Hopkins landed the role of Hannibal Lecter a number of other actors were considered including Gene Hackman, Sean Connery, Derek Jacobi, Daniel Day-Lewis, Robert Duvall, John Hurt and Jack Nicholson.

In 1984 American law enforcement office Robert D. Keppel met with notorious serial killer Ted Bundy to discuss his insights into the at-large Green River Killer. Over the years leading to Bundy's execution in 1989 he would be interviewed many times to offer his theories on the case. The Green River Killer, Gary Ridgway, wouldn't be caught until long after Bundy's death but, according to Keppel, Ted Bundy had been, "Right on the money all the way around," regarding his accurate character profile of

Ridgway. Thomas Harris (author of *The Silence of the Lambs*) was said to have been inspired by Keppel's relationship with Bundy (as detailed in his book *The Riverman: Ted Bundy and I Hunt for the Green River Killer*) and used it as the basis for Clarice Starling and Hannibal Lecter's professional relationship.

Actress Jodie Foster had herself been stalked by a psychopath who would ultimately go to the extreme of attempting to assassinate President Ronald Reagan in order to impress her. John Hinckley Jr. had become obsessed with Foster and the film *Taxi Driver* (1976), in which she played a child prostitute. He signed up for a course at Yale, where Foster was studying, and began to send her love letters and even talk with her on the phone. On March 30th 1981, Hinckley shot at the President as he left the Washington Hilton Hotel. Of the six shots fired only one managed to actually hit Reagan after ricocheting off the side of the armored limousine and puncturing his lung. White House press secretary James Brady was permanently disabled from the attack, having been shot in the head. When Brady died in 2014 his death was ruled as a homicide, 33 years after being shot.

In research for his role as Jack Crawford, actor Scott Glenn was taken under the wing of FBI Special Agent Jack Douglas – the man had who inspired the Jack Crawford character. Glenn was left feeling traumatized after one visit to the FBI Academy at Quantico when Douglas played him an audio recording of a 16 year-old girl being raped and tortured by serial killers Lawrence Bittaker and Roy Norris (The *Tool Box Killers*). The same audiocassette is used as part of the training program at Quantico to desensitize FBI agents to the harsh realities of sexual homicide.

In 2002 there was a documentary series called *Silence of the Lambs* but it had nothing to do with Clarice Starling or Hannibal Lecter. It focused on the lives of farmers after the 2001 foot and mouth outbreak in the UK!

Straw Dogs (1971 – Directed by Sam Peckinpah)

The British Board of Film Classification banned *Straw Dogs* from 1984 to 2002 on account of its rape scenes. Multiple attempts were made to cut the film over the years – James Ferman at the BBFC had suggested three minutes be cut from one of the rape scenes. After the film had been submitted five times it was finally passed uncut in 2002 (notably after James Ferman's retirement from the BBFC in 1999).

Straw Dogs star Dustin Hoffman has said that he found himself blacklisted in Hollywood as a result of apparently upsetting somebody very powerful in the film industry in the early 80's. It has never been revealed exactly what he said, or to whom, but as a result Hoffman was absent from the big screen for over five years. Ironically this was just after Hoffman had starred in *Tootsie* – a film in which he played a failed actor who nobody would hire on account of him being difficult to work with.

<u>Street Trash (1987 – Directed by Jim Muro)</u>

In 2010 Jim Muro announced that he intended to produce a sequel to *Street Trash* but because it was over twenty years since the original film he decided to call it *Street Trash 3*. He said, "I decided it was a better idea just to skip ahead to part three. I hope people will actually be curious about that." As of 2015 Part 3 has yet to materialize. Nor has part 2 for that matter!

<u>The Texas Chain Saw Massacre (1974 – Directed by Tobe Hooper)</u>

The house from the original *The Texas Chain Saw Massacre* was moved from its original location in Round Rock, Texas to Kingsland, Texas, and is now a restaurant called Grand Central Cafe. Note: Don't order the barbeque!

The film struggled to find a distributor and eventually was picked up by Bryanston Distributing Company which was a mafia-run organization headed by Louis "Butchie" Peraino of the Colombo Crime Family. As a result the cast and crew of the film were financially ripped off. Gunnar Hansen (Leatherface) has said that his first royalty check, 9 months after the very successful release of the film, was for $47 and 7 cents.
    "Butchie" lied to the film's producers about the film's profits and when Robert Kuhn (investor and attorney for *The Texas Chain Saw Massacre*) confronted him (and his mafia henchmen) he threated to sue him. "Butchie" told him, "You don't have enough balls to sue me." Eventually the rights were returned to the filmmakers after "Butchie" was arrested on obscenity charges for his involvement

with the film *Deep Throat* (1972).

The film was banned for many years in the UK but was finally released after James Ferman retired from the British Board of Film Classification in 1999. Ferman was notorious in Britain for banning and cutting movies, leading to the introduction of the Video Recordings Act 1984.

The Texas Chainsaw Massacre 2 (1986 – Directed by Tobe Hooper)

Despite Bill Johnson being credited as playing Leatherface, most of the shots containing him holding his iconic chainsaw were filmed with stunt performer Bob Elmore - this was on account of the chainsaw being too heavy for Bill Johnson to lift.

The Thing (1982 – Directed by John Carpenter)

In order to shoot the scene in which Copper's arms are bitten off by Norris's alien infested stomach a stunt performer with no arms (as a result of an industrial accident) was brought in to double as Copper. Special effects artist Rob Bottin also made a mask for the amputee to wear so that it appeared he was the actor playing Copper (Richard Dysart).

John Carpenter considers *The Thing* to be the first in his Apocalypse trilogy with parts two and three being *Prince of Darkness* (1987) and *In the Mouth of Madness* (1994).

Camera operator Raymond Stella was the very willing body double for all of the close-up shots of needles being injected into the character's arms. Kurt Russell jokes on the DVD commentary that

Ray's now in rehab!

30 Days of Night (2007 – Directed by David Slade)

The movie was filmed nowhere near the real city of Barrow in Alaska. It was filmed over seven thousand miles away in Auckland, New Zealand.

30 Days of Night is one of many movies to feature the ubiquitous Wilhelm Scream (an almost comically exaggerated stock sound effect of a man screaming). It was originally recorded to accompany a visual of a man being eaten by an alligator. It has featured in such movies as *Star Wars* (all of them), *Indiana Jones* (all of them), *Poltergeist*, *Howard the Duck*, *Willow*, *Gremlins 2: The New Batch*, *Batman Returns*, *Reservoir Dogs*, *Die Hard: With a Vengeance*, *Toy Story*, *Pirates of the Caribbean*, *Anchorman*, *Tropic Thunder* and *Inglorious Basterds*.

The Town That Dreaded Sundown (1976 – Directed by Charles B. Pierce)

The film is loosely based on a spate of murders that took place in and around Texarkana, Texas, in 1946, known as the *Texarkana Moonlight Murders*. In total five people were murdered by an unidentified killer dubbed the *Phantom Killer* by local newspapers who, like in the movie, wore a burlap sack over his head with two slits for eyes. The attacks would take place roughly within three weeks of each other on quiet, lonely roads where young couples would park-up their cars to make out. Despite over 400 people being brought in for questioning the elusive Phantom Killer was never apprehended.

Even though the residents of Texarkana were initially displeased by the movie's, "Today he still lurks the streets of Texarkana," tagline they have, since 2003, publically screened the film every Halloween in Spring Lake Park – where two of the victims were slain.

Trauma (1976 – Directed by James Kenelm Clarke)

Trauma (also known as *Exposé* and *House on Straw Hill*) is the only British movie to appear on the British Board of Film Classification's Video Nasty List. To this day it is still cut by almost a minute in the UK.

Spandau Ballet's Martin Kemp directed a remake of the movie in 2010 called *Stalker*.

Trick 'r Treat (2007 – Directed by Michael Dougherty)

Special effects legend Stan Winston (*Aliens, Terminator 2, Jurassic Park*) originally optioned Michael Dougherty's screenplay with the intention of hiring different directors to each film a separate story in the movie. George Romero, Tobe Hooper and John Carpenter were all approached with Stan Winston also on board to direct one of the segments. All of the major studios passed on the project stating that the script's content was too old-fashioned and eventually the script ended up being produced by Dougherty's friend, Bryan Singer (Dougherty had worked on the scripts for Singer's *X-Men 2* and *Superman Returns*).

After the film was completed it struggled to get a theatrical release – it was originally slated for an October release in 2007 but was pulled without explanation or reason. Other theatrical release dates were set but none of them manifested. It sat on the shelf for two years before finally going straight to DVD in October 2009. It's unclear what the reasons were for this but it thankfully hasn't affected the very positive reception the film has garnered from horror fans and there's even a sequel in the works.

After the success of *X-Men*, Dougherty made a pitch for *The Goonies 2* to both Steven Spielberg and Richard Donner, who both loved it. They took the project to Warner Bros. who said they weren't interested in a *Goonies* franchise. Dougherty has said it was really bizarre to see someone saying, "No," to Steven Spielberg and made him realize that it clearly doesn't matter who you are in Hollywood, "If you have a project that you're passionate about, you're always going to have a tough time getting it made," he said.

The mischievous character of Sam from *Trick 'r Treat* was first introduced in Dougherty's 1996 short animated film *Season's Greetings* in which the viewer is misled into thinking that a little boy (Sam) in a Jack o'lantern burlap-sack mask is murdered in a dark alleyway by a child killer – it transpires that the opposite is true and that Sam has killed the man instead. Some of the blood on Sam's face at the end was actually Dougherty's blood – he had cut his hand whilst animating it and decided to use it!

The Uninvited (2009 – Directed by The Guard Brothers)

The film is inspired by an old Korean folktale called Janghwa Hongryeon jeon, which literally means 'The Story of Janghwa and Hongryeon'. The tale tells of two sisters, one of whom is murdered by her evil stepmother and stepbrother, the other commits suicide as a result of her death. The girls return as ghosts to kill every new Mayor in the village until one brave Mayor confronts them. The ghosts explain the truth about their deaths and the stepmother and stepmother are sentenced to death. The folktale has served as the basis for a number of Korean feature films and *The Uninvited* marked its first Hollywood adaptation.

Vacancy (2007 – Directed by Nimród Antal)

In order to advertise and promote the movie the filmmakers set up a toll-free phone number for the fictional Pine-Wood Motel from the film. When called, the voice of actor Frank Whaley (the motel proprietor) would inform you of the motel's *killer* deals and how they are *slashing* prices – all of this accompanied by the sounds of screaming in the background.

The motel set was built on the same sound stage (stage 15 at Sony Pictures Studios, formally MGM studios) that the *Wizard of Oz* (1939) was filmed on.

84

<u>V/H/S 2 (2013 – Directed by Simon Barrett, Adam Wingard, Eduardo Sánchez, Gregg Hale, Timo Tjahjanto, Gareth Huw Evans and Jason Eisener)</u>

Having popularized the found-footage genre with *The Blair Witch Project* director Eduardo Sánchez admits he felt nervous participating in the film. In an interview for Bloody Disgusting he said, "We're kind of like the godfather's of found-footage… man, ours better not be the fucking worst one!"

<u>The Wicker Man (1973 – Directed by Robin Hardy)</u>

There was a sequel-of-sorts made in 2011 called *The Wicker Tree*, which had experienced many financial setbacks before finally going into production in July 2009 – it had been conceived back in 2002. Christopher Lee was set to have a much larger role in the film but due to a back injury he incurred on the set of *The Resident* (2011) his participation was reduced to a small cameo. Robin Hardy, now in his 80's, is currently prepping a third *Wicker Man* movie entitled *The Wrath of the Gods*. The same financial setbacks seem to be plaguing the production – filming was originally set to begin in 2011.

A number of different versions of the film have been released over the years. When the original film was edited and presented to British Lion Films they weren't sure exactly what to do with it, being slightly baffled by its morbid content and tone. The filmmakers were ordered to cut it down in the hope that they could at least distribute it as part of a double-bill package with *Don't Look Now* (1973). Many years later a Director's Cut version was released that contained previously excised footage that had been thought to be lost but was obtained from legendary American Producer Roger Corman, who had been sent an earlier cut of the film in the 70's. In 2013 Robin Hardy re-edited the movie creating something of a hybrid of the earlier releases – calling it *The Final Cut*, which used a print of the film that had recently been unearthed at the Harvard Film Archive. Even though he says it's not quite the same as his lost original version Hardy says, "It crucially restores the story order to that which I had originally intended." The long-standing rumor is that Robin Hardy's original version of the movie was used as landfill and is buried under the M3 Motorway in England but no one has ever been able to substantiate this claim with any evidence.

A music festival has been held every year in Scotland in the same area that *The Wicker Man* was shot, in Dumfries and Galloway. The Wickerman Festival has hosted an eclectic mix of bands over the years including The Scissor Sisters, KT Tunstall, Fun Lovin' Criminals, The Human League and The Stranglers. The festival culminates with the burning of a giant wicker man statue.

The wooden remnants of the wicker man's legs at Burrow Head, near Isle of Whithorn, were stolen in 2006 having remained encased in concrete, inscribed with WM - 1972, at the location for over 30 years.

Wolf Creek (2007 – Directed by Greg McLean)

Although the movie claims to be based on true events it is not based solely on one specific story, rather an amalgamation of real events, murders and disappearances that took place in the Australian Outback. One inspiration was said to be the story of British tourists Peter Falconio and Joanne Lees that took place in the Northern Territory two thousand miles away from the Wolfe Creek National Park, near Barrow Creek. They encountered a mechanic called Bradley John Murdoch whilst travelling at night on the Stuart Highway. Murdoch had noticed they were having engine trouble and as Falconio accompanied Murdoch to look at the vehicle Lees heard a gunshot. Murdoch tied up Lees but she was able to escape and after hiding for a few hours she flagged down a truck and made it to safety. Despite Falconio's body having never been found Murdoch was captured and found guilty of his murder. The release of *Wolf Creek* was delayed in the Northern Territory on account of its potential to influence the outcome of the court case.

The other influence is said to be the Backpacker Murders in New South Wales in the early 1990's. Serial killer Ivan Milat was convicted of torturing and murdering seven young backpackers before burying them in shallow graves in the Belanglo New State Forest. The victim's bodies displayed evidence of numerous gunshot wounds, multiple stabbings, strangulation, severe beating and, in one case, decapitation.

Wrong Turn 6: Last Resort (2014 – Directed by Valeri Milev)

The producers of *Wrong Turn 6* made the rather dubious decision to include the photograph of an actual missing person in the film without any approval whatsoever. The photograph had been provided to the press to help locate 66 year-old Stacia Purcell from County Wexford in Ireland (who was later found dead, having suffered from a heart attack and falling into a river). When Purcell's family were informed that her image had been used to depict a missing 81 year-old man in the horror flick they took legal action against the film's distributor, 20th Century Fox Home Entertainment. As a result of the court case all DVD and Blu-ray copies of the film were recalled from distribution.

Xtro (1982 – Directed by Harry Bromley Davenport)

In 2014 social media sites went crazy over a photograph of an alleged skin-walker creature stood on all fours by a roadside in Lybrook, New Mexico. A skin-walker is a legendary Native American tale of a person who has the supernatural ability to turn themselves into any creature they desire. Having frightened people online and featured on local TV news stations, the photo of the creepy looking creature was eventually debunked and revealed to have been lifted from the scene of the alien on a woodland road from *Xtro*.

Young Frankenstein (1974 – Directed by Mel Brooks)

The Aerosmith hit *Walk this Way* was inspired by a scene in *Young Frankenstein*. During a break from recording the *Toys in the Attic* album the band went to see the film in Times Square and found the scene with Marty Feldman ushering Gene Wilder on the train station particularly funny. Whilst they were chatting about it later and quoting Feldman's, "Walk this way," line, producer Jack Douglas said, "Hey, that's a great title for a song!" And the rest is history!

Zodiac (2007 – Directed by David Fincher)

The film shot in a number of the real locations where the Zodiac Killer events took place including Lake Berryessa where Bryan Hartnell and Cecelia Shepard were attacked in 1969. According to Robert Graysmith (author of *Zodiac*) whilst they were filming at Lake Berryessa director David Fincher seemed unsure that they were in the actual spot where the crime had taken place. He walked over to a different area, put his head to the ground, felt the dirt and gravel and listened to the traffic before walking back over to the crew. He then informed Detective Ken Narlow (who worked on the actual case and was an advisor on the film) that he thought the place he'd just looked at was the correct location. Narlow looked around and retorted to Fincher, "My God, you're right! I took you to the wrong spot!" That David Fincher is a spooky guy!

Zombie aka Zombie Flesh Eaters (1979 – Directed by Lucio Fulci)

The film has many alternative titles across the world including... *Island of the Flesh-Eaters, Zombi, Zombi 2, Zombies, Island of the Living Dead* and *Woodoo*.

Across the globe various films have been marketed as being sequels to Fulci's film although none of them are actually true sequels and most have absolutely no connection with the original:

In the UK...
Zombie (1979) became *Zombie Flesh Eaters*
Zombi 3 (1988) became *Zombie Flesh Eaters 2*
After Death (1989) became *Zombie Flesh Eaters 3*

In Italy...
George A. Romero's *Dawn of the Dead* (1978) became *Zombi*
Zombie aka *Zombie Flesh Eaters* (1979) became *Zombi 2*
Zombi 3 (1988) was simply called *Zombi 3*

In Germany...
Dawn of the Dead (1978) became *Zombie*
Day of the Dead (1985) became *Zombie 2*
Zombi 3 (1988) became *Zombie 3*
Strangely enough Fulci's 1979 *Zombie* isn't included – this was released separately as *Woodoo*

In Thailand...
Zombie (1979) became *Zombie Flesh Eaters*
Zombi 3 (1988) became *Zombie Flesh Eaters 2*
After Death (1989) became *Zombie Flesh Eaters 3*
Killing Birds (1988) became *Zombie Flesh Eaters 4*

In America...

Zombie aka *Zombie Flesh Eaters* (1979) was simply *Zombie*
Zombi 3 (1988) became *Zombie 3*
After Death (1989) became *Zombie 4*
Killing Birds (1988) became *Zombie 5*
America seemed to skip calling anything *Zombie 2*!

In order to shoot the incredible zombie vs. shark scene a real shark was used. The actor who was scheduled to play the zombie in the sequence wisely claimed to be ill on the day of the shoot and the shark's trainer, Ramon Bravo, agreed to take his place. In order to get so close to the shark it had been fed horse meat and tranquilizers prior to shooting. I think I would have called in sick too!

Zombieland (2009 – Directed by Ruben Fleischer)

Multiple versions of the script were written to incorporate different potential celebrity cameos. Initially Patrick Swayze had been sought but after he became ill the filmmakers approached a variety of other stars including Sylvester Stallone, Jean-Claude Van Damme, The Rock, Joe Pesci, Mark Hamill and Matthew McConaughey. Just days before the scene was due to be filmed McConaughey backed out, leaving the production with no celebrity. The script was hastily re-written without a cameo scene, fearing that they would be unable to find a willing participant. Star Woody Harrelson suggested approaching Bill Murray, informing the writers of the best method to contact the elusive actor. Thankfully the script successfully found its way to him in the nick of time and Murray was on set just two days later.

In 2013 a TV pilot of *Zombieland* was produced for Amazon Studios, written by the movie's original writers Rhett Reese and Paul Wernick. When the show was dropped after just one episode, Reese tweeted on his Twitter account, "Sad for everyone involved... I'll never understand the vehement hate the pilot received from die-hard *Zombieland* fans. You guys successfully hated it out of existence."

Epilogue

In this spirit of this book I feel that it is appropriate to come clean with the true story of Ellen Mort. Whenever I publish a new book or promote my books online I have always used the same biography (which can, indeed, be viewed at the beginning of this book). Okay, so there's no direct evidence to support that my great-great-great-grandmother was a serial killer, however it is true that she married six times (even though I've always written five, on account of the last one being in America – you'll see why in a moment) and one of her married names was Ellen Mort. Her birth name was Ellen Byrom and her other married surnames were Ellison, Robinson, Hunt, Wilkinson and Baldwin. Ellen wasn't actually born in Liverpool, though she did later live there – she was actually born in Ashton-in-Makerfield in Manchester, England in 1840. The Liverpool connection is very interesting though. In the city of Liverpool in 1884, sisters Catherine Flannagan and Margaret Higgins were both hanged (at the same time) for the murder of Margaret's husband, Thomas Higgins. They had poisoned him using arsenic extracted from commonly available flypaper and had collected on five burial society insurance policies that they had taken out on him prior to his death. Thomas Higgins' brother suspected foul play and a full autopsy was performed on Thomas's body that indeed concluded that he had died as a result of arsenic poisoning. Flannagan and Higgins would later be labeled *The Black Widows of Liverpool* and many other deaths would be subsequently linked to them.

So, this is where Ellen Mort comes into the story – she lived in Liverpool at the same time as the Black Widow sisters and modern investigations have uncovered a potential network of black widows - all of whom were quite possibly murdering people they knew to collect on the insurance money. Ellen Mort's whopping six marriages (especially during a time when it was very uncommon for women to marry more than once – six is still pretty uncommon these day!) makes her very, very suspect! Okay, so she didn't *violently butcher* them but it's difficult, under the circumstances, not to surmise that Ellen was somehow involved in this web of murderous women. She was in the right place at the right time - and all of her husbands did die. I'm just putting two and two together!

The final part of the Ellen Mort tale is also true, that she did move to Salt Lake City, Utah and (so far) my family has been unable to determine exactly what happened to her after that.

So, I hoped that's cleared that up! More than that, I sincerely hope that you have enjoyed reading this book - I had a lot of fun writing and researching it and finding out about all these fascinating tales from some of my favorite horror movies. Incredibly, for myself, whilst researching *The Wicker Man* (1973) I discovered that I had unknowingly visited the beach that features at the end of the movie whilst on holiday in Scotland in 2014. As a horror fanatic I'm almost ashamed to admit that I was completely oblivious I was traipsing along the shoreline where one of the most iconic horror movies of all time was filmed! In my defense, St. Ninian's Cave in Whithorn fails to acknowledge the movie on the information plaque outside the cave – which I think is a far worse travesty than my ignorance!

Well, that's all, folks! Happy horror viewing to y'all!

Acknowledgments

A very special thanks to the following people for their help with the research and writing of this book – Peter Atherton, Ed Boase, Sean Clark, Scott Derrickson, Carl V. Dupre, Scott Glosserman, Nathan Head, Ben Loyd-Holmes, Susan Lisbeth Kaufman, Adam Marcus, Derek Mears, Adam Spinks, Neal Marshall Stevens, Marcus Nispel, Rex Piano, Jim Proser and Katherine and Graham Hamer (aka Mum and Dad).

Bibliography

Primary Sources

Websites/Magazines/Newspapers:

Texas Monthly
Wikipedia
IMDb
Facebook
Twitter
ChillerTV
YouTube
eBay
Lynchnet.com
People.com
mirror.co.uk
yahoo.com
ukyahoo.com
stackexchange.com
empireonline.com
deathandtaxesmag.com
Maxlevelgeek.com
Cult Oddities
thedailybeast.com
ABC news
cracked.com
moviepilot.com
SFX Magazine
toprightnews.com
cropseylegend.com
independent.co.uk
theguardian.com
The New York Observer
hollywoodreporter.com
artclassy.com

filmbuffonline.com
bbfc.co.uk
ihorror.com
warrens.net
The News Tribune
The Wichita Eagle
screenrant.com
thefw.com
realitysandwich.com
the-artifice.com
wegotthiscovered.com
fridaythe13thfilms.com
fridaythe13thfranchise.com
lovehorror.co.uk
wow247.co.uk
laweekly.com
loopnet.com
boxofficemojo.com
bloody-disgusting.com
dailymail.co.uk
filmschoolrejects.com
iconsoffright.com
travelcreepster.com
mentalfloss.com
hauntedamericatours.com
thecolonialtheatre.com
Miskatonic Books Blog
wsj.com
compleatseanbean.com
nzherald.co.nz
horrorsociety.com
outback-australia-travel-secrets.com
encyclopediaofarkansas.net
i09.com
krqe.com
indiewire.com
prisonplanet.com

Premiere Magazine
news.bbc.co.uk
bradbittpress.com
dailydread.com
maths.tcd.ie
thehollywoodinterview.blogspot.co.uk
empireonline.com
movie-censorship.com
nbcnews.com
csun.edu
thiskevin.blogspot.co.uk
nothingtoseehere.net
avclub.com
uk.complex.com
ibtimes.co.uk
horror.wikia.com
kickstarter.com
filmscouts.com
independent.ie
vulture.com
tested.com
alienseries.wordpress.com
halloweenlove.com
theraffon.net
profanitymaybe.blogspot.co.uk
houseofhorrors.com
murderpedia.org
cbc.ca
The New Jersey Herald
movieblog.mtv.com

<u>Books:</u>

The Hellraiser Films and Their Legacy by Paul Kane; *Crystal Lake Memories: The Complete History of Friday the 13th* by Peter Bracke; *Clive Barker's A–Z of Horror* compiled by Stephen Jones; *Crazy River* by Richard Grant; *The Evil Dead Companion* by Bill Warren; *Hello, He Lied* by Linda Obst; *Life and Laughing: My Story* by Michael McIntyre; *The Jaws Log* by Carl Gottlieb; *The Black Widows of Liverpool* by Angela Brabin.

Killian H. Gore will return in

Digging Deeper: Incredible Horror Movie Facts Part II

COMING SOON!!!

Morning Jogger

by Killian H. Gore

MORNING JOGGER

Two months ago the local newspaper, delivered to each and every household in the Alaskan town of Bontykan, contained a familiar headline.

There had been another suicide.

It made the total twelve in less than a year. With a population of around eight thousand it was an unusually high amount even for urban Alaska. The state was known to have some of the highest suicide rates, not just in America, but also the world. The long hours of darkness, the extreme cold and isolation were strong contributing factors. Riley Billings didn't think about such things when he moved to the town for seven weeks. The twenty five year old Canadian actor had taken on a supporting role in a horror movie *Skeleton Lake* being filmed in the town. It was a good role and a decent budget, in the millions. Low millions, but still millions.

Riley wasn't an enormously well known actor, aside from his role in the short-lived cult sci-fi TV show *Aerial Gold* a few years ago. He was, now, more the type of actor who had regular work and hoped that the next project would be the big one. He felt the same way about *Skeleton Lake*. It had a good cast and an established director in Adam Vanderbilt and, in fact, he didn't really care if it become the next *Halloween*, *Friday the 13th* or *A Nightmare on Elm Street*, he was young and in a new town with money in his pocket. He had relative success, wealth and his health, which he took good care of, and wherever he found himself he would religiously take a morning jog. It wasn't like there would be screaming fans chasing after him - even if he was *that* famous he doubted many people would be up at six in the morning to hound him. With such early call times for film shoots he had to be up even earlier to go running.

Riley had arrived a week before the start of the shoot and would pay the hotel bill himself until the start of filming. He wasn't required until the weekend, when they would be having a read-through. If his schedule allowed for it he would often arrive early and spend some time exploring the new location his vibrant career took him to. It was an exiting way to live - always on the road, just like a rock star. He wished he had the talent to be an actual rock star but he could only strum the chords that everyone else can strum. He claimed his fingers were too chunky to play guitar; too athletic. At least that was his excuse.

On his first night in Bontykan he went to the first local bar he eyed, The Barley Inn, which was just around the corner from his hotel. He'd hoped to strike up some sort of conversation with somebody – even the bar staff, but nobody seemed interested in the movie star. It didn't really help that there was an Acoustic Night taking place with one gravely singer after another damaging their guitar strings and vocal chords. Everywhere around him were signs for the famous local beer, Despo-Ice, made with the glacier-fed water from the nearby Lake Despo. It was the town's main export so they certainly had the right to plaster its imagery all over the walls, bar and tables. Riley drank a few Despo-Ice beers as he sat at a table close to the stage - a small cordoned off area at the far end of the smoky room. By sitting there he'd hoped to at least converse with some of the musicians and perhaps perform a song himself. Like all average guitar heroes he had his party piece: *Dead or Alive* by Bon Jovi. Under normal circumstances he was a little ropey with the opening riff, but after a few beers he would be dreadful so it was just as well that the opportunity never arose. Feeling a little crushed and lonely he left the bar early and headed back to his hotel room.

The air was crisply cold outside and complemented the warmth of both the alcohol and the heat of the Barley Inn flawlessly. Upon arrival at the Maybole Hotel he asked at the reception if there was anywhere he could get some cartons of fresh orange and some bananas for the morning.

"Those will all be served as part of the breakfast here, Sir."

"Yes, I realize that. I just tend to get up pretty early. I was wondering if I could get some now. Or... if there's somewhere in town maybe I..."

"Oh no, Sir, that's quite all right. Will Sir be requiring a wake up call?"

"Hey, no bud. No, that's cool. So..." Riley still hadn't received the answer he wanted.

"And of course we will have the... was it orange juice?"

"Yeah. And bananas would be great if you've got them?"

"I will check with the kitchen but I'm sure it will be no problem, Sir." Aiden, the immaculately attired charming receptionist gave his best smile. Unlike the occupants of the Barley Inn, Aiden knew who Riley was. He was a fan of *Ariel Gold* – even though it had only lasted one season it had a substantial following among sci-fi fans. He also knew that the actor was here to shoot a feature film. Everyone at the hotel knew about the feature film coming to town.

"Great. Thanks," Riley said before turning and pacing over to the elevator.

Even though he wouldn't be required to rise early until the following week, Riley still liked to get up early for his morning run. Primarily this was because he enjoyed the feeling that the world belonged to him at that time. Aside from the dog-walking crowd, it was rare, no matter where he was, that he would see many other people, unless it was in a big city.

He set the alarm on his mobile phone for half past five and figured on starting his run at six, after consuming the fruit that was hopefully on its way up to his room. There were two voice mails and a few text messages to deal with before he set his alarm. There were always messages. Being around so many film shoots he had gotten accustomed to either turning his cell phone off or having it on silent. So many of the calls were superfluous anyway. His agent's message told him about a sci-fi convention in Connecticut on the upcoming weekend. He'd failed to state it was because Danson Glass had dropped out of the *Aerial Gold* signing. Riley was smart enough to realize the likely truth. He'd call tomorrow to decline, using the perfectly rational excuse of it being too far away – *I'm in Alaska! Working! You dipshit!*

Aiden knocked on the door, proudly holding onto a small fruit basket and a carton of orange juice from the kitchens. The door swung open.

"Ah! Hey, that's great. Thanks, dude," Riley said, without giving Aiden a chance to introduce the goods.

110

"That's no problem, Sir." Aiden handed the basket and carton over to Riley, keeping his warm smile intact the whole time. "If there's anything else…"

"No, no. This is great, man.

"And you're sure you don't need a wake up call? It's not a problem."

"Thanks, no, I'm okay," Riley began to close the door.

"Okay, well, goodnight, Sir."

"Yeah," Riley finished shutting the door. Even though he appreciated the fruit, he tired of people being falsely nice to him. He couldn't even distinguish if people were sincere anymore. Unfortunately Aiden was sincere. It didn't matter.

Riley undressed and got into the cold bed. It wouldn't be long until the beer took him away to unconsciousness. He placed the phone on the empty bedside table and clicked off the light above the bed. The television remained on, set to the movie channel. A dumb comedy film played that he'd seen a hundred times before. It was comforting in the foreign environment and he couldn't sleep without the flickering light and familiar sounds provided by a familiar movie. He watched it for a few minutes before closing his eyes and turning onto his side. He smiled as he heard the same jokes in the film that he always laughed at.

At half past five Riley's mobile phone dutifully sounded its alarm. He awoke immediately and grabbed it, wanting to stop the awful vibrations it made on the hollow bedside table. It sounded like some sort of electronic thunder.

Frightening. Intrusive in the otherwise silent room.

The television was on, as it had been all night - it was an animated film that he wasn't familiar with, not at the moment anyway, much too early to determine.

He held his eyes wide open and looked around the room. It was the same moment he had every morning, the moment when he considered putting the phone back down and pulling the covers over his head and postponing the morning run, indefinitely. But as he watched the screen for a minute or so, eyes wide, face stretched, mouth wide open, tongue sticking all the way out, he knew he was soon going to be on his feet. The need to urinate would guarantee that.

"Holy Schnike!" he said to himself as he pushed the duvet off the bed and climbed onto the soft carpet.

Outside the hotel it was cold and dark. Riley sucked in the chilled air through his nose and breathed out hard through his mouth. To boost his energy levels he'd already had half the carton of orange and a banana in his room, leaving the rest for when he returned. He was glad that the smiley bellboy (or whatever he was) hadn't been on the desk to greet him. It had been a much older man with scruffy, wild hair. Riley didn't perceive it as odd though, he was in the movie business, after all.

Odd was his life. Odd was everywhere!

Having already done his stretching after a quick read through of the *Skeleton Lake* script on the toilet, Riley took a few deep breaths, taking the cold weather into his system before starting to lightly jog. He headed off onto the empty main

112

street, running into the middle of the road. There was no traffic around.

In the distance he could see lavish suburban properties up in the tree adorned hills. He opted to run towards them, away from the shops, bars and businesses that dominated the central area of town - the woods beckoned. The whole town of Bontykan was coated by trees. They surrounded it, cradled it. The area was quite spectacular. A pleasure to run through, even in the dreary early morning light.

All of the houses seemed completely different from one other. Riley was fascinated by them, hardly even looking at the road ahead of him as he ran leisurely by. His pace became more labored as he found himself running uphill. He could feel the sweat running down his back as he ascended the idyllic streets. The freezing cold weather slammed into his face though his head was kept warm by his Chinchilla Trooper hat. The rest of his body was wrapped up in a thick-layered tracksuit.

He turned into a new street, Whithorn Road. Ahead of him were six more houses, again all differently designed, leading up to the woods. Immediately he noticed that someone was watching him out of the upstairs window of the first house. Riley gave a tiny smile as he continued to run. The child had been staring at him with both of his hands pressed to the glass. Odd, yes, but he *was* used to odd after all.

But things got stranger.

The second house, the upstairs window.

Two children, a boy and a girl both at the window. Hands pressed to the glass, raised in the same way as the first child, fingers spread wide.

Their faces were as expressionless as the first child's.

This time Riley didn't smile. He felt a tad annoyed. It was as if someone had told them he was in town and would be running at this time. To him they seemed more like annoying fans, just like that Aiden guy at the hotel. But unlike Aiden, there was no smiling to be seen here. They were just watching him.

He approached the third house.

Another face. A little older this time. A teenage boy, his hands pressed to the glass. Watching.

Riley shook his head in disbelief and upped his speed in spite of the uphill struggle. He took in a deep lungful of air and passed the fourth house. He didn't really want to look but couldn't help himself.

There were three of them. All different ages. Two girls and a boy. Every one of them watching him.

He considered waving, thinking that it must be some kind of collective of fans, maybe of *Aerial Gold* - the show did have a pretty good cult following, but it seemed rather far fetched to believe there was such a collective of fans in one small street deep in Alaska.

The last two houses were across the road from each other, unlike the others that had been more spaced out along Whithorn Road.

And there they were again in both houses. In the left house one of them looked more Riley's age. Another was just a little kid, the other a teen. Two older faces stared at him from the other house. Every one of them at the upstairs windows staring blankly down at him, their hands pressed to the glass.

114

The woods ahead brought with them sanctuary. At least in there he would be free of the strange people in the windows gawking at him. Even though he'd spent the majority of his life working in film and television he couldn't recall ever having seen such a strange sight. Even the bizarre film by Rip Dutham, in which he'd played the victim of a deranged Librarian who'd killed him with a razorblade stamper for returning his book late wasn't as weird - and everyone on that film was on acid! That was how he felt now. Like he'd taken something and bad things were happening. Inexplicable things.

He ran past the last house on the left and into the woods, not wanting to look back down at the freaky street. The rough dirt path he jogged onto took an immediate turn to the right and the view of the houses was blocked by the lush Sitka spruce and mountain hemlock trees. He made the decision there and then that he would take a different route back to the hotel. For now he would continue with his morning jog and forget about the peculiar images. The rising sun had illuminated the surroundings since his excursion commenced, but inside the woods it was still quite dark. He wasn't the type of person to find such things disturbing though even if he was alone and in such foreboding light conditions.

But when the wild haired man from the hotel desk stepped out from the trees in front of him he became frightened in an instant, feeling a rollercoaster lunge grip his heart.

It wasn't his crazy hair, or his frenzied eyes that chilled him, it was his sudden appearance from out of the shadowy trees. Although he had very little time to think he assumed it must have been some sort of emergency at the hotel. There was no time to speculate what kind of emergency could possibly have occurred because the hotel clerk pulled out something from behind his back.

It was a broken-off tree branch.

No words had time to formulate.

There was no time to react either.

The branch was swung at Riley's head with a horribly hollow *thunk* and the actor fell to the rough, cold ground.

When Riley awoke he was back in his hotel room where the wild haired man, Leland, was holding a gun to his head.

"Good morning, Mr. Billings. I trust the fruit basket was to your satisfaction?"

Was this guy kidding?

Riley looked at the bedside table. His mobile phone was no longer alone on there - it was kept company by a large bottle of vodka and two pill containers. He couldn't read the label from where he lay but he thought they were probably Aspirin.

Looking up from the table he noticed Aiden was also in the room. He walked over to the bottle of vodka, smiling as usual.

"So what did you think of *Skeleton Lake*? I wrote some of it myself," Leland said, rather conversationally. "Up to Hollywood standards? Well, I suppose it must have been or you wouldn't have come here. Maybe we'll send it to the film studios," he said with a smirk.

Aiden screwed the lid off the bottle of vodka and poured out a full glass. *Glug, glug, glug, glug, glug.*

Leland was still smiling. He looked very pleased with himself.

Riley tried to move and realized that his arms were bound behind his back and his legs, too, were tied. *Oh shit.*

Aiden opened one of the pill containers. Leland walked over closer to Riley, reiterating the fact that he had a gun and that it was pointing at the young actor's head.

"You can do this voluntarily, Mr. Billings," Leland left a pause. Clearly for dramatic effect - no wonder this psycho had been so good at writing a movie script, "or we can wedge a funnel down your throat and force it down."

"I don't understand. What... what are you...?"

"We brought you here, Mr. Billings. You are to be the thirteenth suicide in our town."

"What... the what...?"

Leland turned to Aiden with an inane grin. "I guess it really *is* unlucky for some!"

"Listen, I have money... I... you..."

"We don't want your money. I think you *know* that already. This isn't some cliché scene from one of your movies. You can't talk your way out of it like James Bond," Leland nodded at Aiden, glancing at the pills.

The smiling bellboy had a handful of the Aspirins in one hand and a glass of vodka in the other.

Riley looked over to him. "No ice?" It was a ridiculous time to attempt humor but pleading obviously wasn't the solution.

The pills were below Riley's mouth. He glanced down at them. There were about six tablets. They looked so innocent. Like little sweets, but there was nothing sweet about them or the situation. These men wanted him to kill himself. And he had no idea why.

Aiden pushed the pills toward Riley's mouth and tipped them slightly.

"Come on, Mr. Billings. This is going to happen no matter what you do or say."

"But why!? Please! You *have* to tell me why!"

"No. No we don't."

Aiden tipped the pills a little more but Riley kept his mouth tightly closed.

"Get the funnel, Aiden."

The morning newspaper, The Bontykan Daily News, was delivered once again to every house in the town the following day. The headline read:

THIRTEENTH SUICIDE – HOLLYWOOD ACTOR FOUND DEAD

Another apparent suicide has taken place in the town center area of Bontykan.

Twenty-five year old Canadian-born Riley Billings, a well-known actor from Hollywood, was found in his hotel room bed yesterday evening with sleeping pills and vodka nearby, police said. Though his death is thought to be the result of a handgun blast to the head. It is not clear at this time why the Aerial Gold actor was in Alaska but it is speculated that he had become depressed recently with his acting career.

A post-mortem examination is scheduled for tomorrow.

His agent, Terry Raedler has confirmed that Billing's had been contacted on the day before his death concerning an appearance at a Connecticut science fiction fan convention.

His death is now the thirteenth suicide in the town of Bontykan in under a year.

Police have declined to comment on any links between the deaths stating only that they are not treating the spate of apparent suicides as suspicious.

Printed in Great Britain
by Amazon